"Megan Westra's *Born Again and Again* offers an especially winsome example of a new post-evangelical spirituality and ethic that is emerging in our time, especially among a massive cohort of young Christians. Westra's lovely book mixes her own story and reflections with those of many others she has invited to speak within its pages. I am glad to encounter this book. It gives me hope for the future."

David P. Gushee, professor of Christian ethics and director of the Center for Theology and Public Life at Mercer University and author of *After Evangelicalism: The Path to a New Christianity*

"Megan Westra's story is my story—and the story of so many who were born into a transactional version of Christianity and tried our very best to live it in the world. What she found, and what I hope for all of us, is a faith rooted in deep connection and relationship, a way of being Christian in the world that values and honors the voices of all God's people. If you are doing the work of reimagining your faith, read this book. You'll find hope and inspiration here."

Amy K. Butler, public theologian and former senior minister of the Riverside Church

"What could the future of Christianity look like in America? Pastor Megan Westra has been living it in her community and now shares what she's learned in this wide-ranging, historically informed, and hopeful book that centers diverse voices and helps us see new possibilities for the church. This isn't an attack on what has failed. Westra's strength is in her call to expand our view of what the church can be in the future with a personal, communal, and public faith."

Ed Cyzewski, author of *Reconnect: Spiritual Restoration from Digital Distraction* and *Flee, Be Silent, Pray: Ancient Prayers for Anxious Christians*

"This book should be required reading for every Christian! Megan Westra's masterful biblical and theological work unravels and uproots the vision of salvation as merely personal and not communal, as verbal assent but not sacrificial, and as emotional but not transformational. She lights the way forward for her readers, revealing a faith patterned after the life of Jesus, and a salvation not just for the self but for the flourishing of everyone. If you have been left empty and disappointed by a personal relationship with Jesus that failed to address the injustices in the world, this book will challenge and encourage you. Westra has gifted us with a robust and clarifying doctrine of salvation, pointing us in the direction of liberation, not just for the individual but also for a church bound by the empire."

Karen González, author of The God Who Sees: Immigrants, the Bible, and the Journey to Belong

"*Born Again and Again* nails it! Megan Westra's artistically woven words contrast the journey of American Christianity and its history of individualism and capitalism with the teachings and life of Jesus as well as Old Testament journeys of God's people. She incorporates interludes of her own personal journey, which includes insights from present-day scholars and past theologians. She also gives a way forward that creates in the reader a love for Jesus. Her writing is compelling and page turning. In a sense, as I was reading it, I was struck with the prophetic tones. A must-read."

Jo Anne Lyon, ambassador and former general superintendent of the Wesleyan Church and founder of World Hope International

"From a bird's-eye view and with a particular lens, Megan Westra invites us to look again at the implications of being the church in the US, not as individuals 'saved from hell' but as a communal people saved for God and bearing public witness to God's transforming presence and purposes for the world. On the canvas of her Christian experience and against the backdrop of US church history, Westra paints panoramic and local scenes of 'unlearning and returning' that are simultaneously insightful, troubling, challenging, and uplifting. For churches seeking to rediscover their 'born again' life in Jesus' cruciform, other-oriented gospel—and to be saved from consumerist narratives embedded in North American evangelicalism—Westra's passionate, practical book is an able companion."

Cherith Fee Nordling, associate professor of theology at Northern Seminary

BORN AGAIN and AGAIN

MEGAN K. WESTRA

BORN AGAIN and AGAIN

JESUS' CALL TO RADICAL TRANSFORMATION

HERALD
PRESS

Harrisonburg, Virginia

Herald Press
PO Box 866, Harrisonburg, Virginia 22803
www.HeraldPress.com

Library of Congress Cataloging-in-Publication Data
Names: Westra, Megan K., author.
Title: Born again and again : Jesus' call to radical transformation / Megan
    K. Westra.
Description: Harrisonburg, Virginia : Herald Press, [2020] | Includes
    bibliographical references.
Identifiers: LCCN 2019059961 (print) | LCCN 2019059962 (ebook) | ISBN
    9781513806747 (paperback) | ISBN 9781513806754 (hardcover) | ISBN
    9781513806761 (ebook)
Subjects: LCSH: Evangelicalism--United States--History. | Christianity and
    politics--United States--History. | Church and social problems--United
    States. | Jesus Christ--Example. | Salvation--Christianity.
Classification: LCC BR1642.U5 .W475 2020 (print) | LCC BR1642.U5 (ebook)
    | DDC 261.8--dc23
LC record available at https://lccn.loc.gov/2019059961
LC ebook record available at https://lccn.loc.gov/2019059962

Study guides are available for many Herald Press titles at www.HeraldPress.com.

BORN AGAIN AND AGAIN
© 2020 by Herald Press, Harrisonburg, Virginia 22803. 800-245-7894.
    All rights reserved.
Library of Congress Control Number: 2019059961
International Standard Book Number: 978-1-5138-0674-7 (paperback);
    978-1-5138-0675-4 (hardcover); 978-1-5138-0676-1 (ebook)
Printed in United States of America
Cover and interior design by Reuben Graham

Unless otherwise noted, Scripture text is quoted, with permission, from the
New Revised Standard Version, © 1989, Division of Christian Education of the
National Council of Churches of Christ in the United States of America.

24 23 22 21 20   10 9 8 7 6 5 4 3 2 1

CONTENTS

FOREWORD

It is the highest honor when someone takes in a concept, theory, or viewpoint that you offered the world so deeply that it becomes an integral part of the way they conceptualize, theorize, and view the world . . . and then they move it forward. Megan Westra has done exactly that in this beautiful and insight-filled book.

Perhaps my favorite line in the pages that follow is the very first: "I was four years old the first time I got saved." Profoundly particular stories, worldviews, political allegiances, histories, struggles, theologies, and ecclesiologies are held in those eleven words. In those words I see white evangelical faith, mostly rural or suburban, family-oriented, but steeped in the insular concern of who's in and who's out, and in a commitment to God and country—first as Democrats, and then as the Republicans that they became in the 1980s. This faith followed the tide of white evangelical support for Ronald

Reagan's American dawn—the dawn of a post–civil rights era that reclaimed white power and reasserted white Christian sovereignty. I see the granddaughters and daughters of white sharecroppers and fishermen and coal miners, some who scattered north by northwest in their own great migration at the turn of the twentieth century, and others who fled west to escape the Dust Bowl. I see white churches—literally painted white—with high steeples, pillars flanking double-door entrances, and hymn numbers slid into wooden slats behind church organs. I see all-white church communities that have played and fought and married each other for generations. Finally, I see a cultural kind of Christianity—caught by osmosis—with little to no likeness to the physically brown, politically black Jesus of the actual text.

By naming Jesus as physically brown, I recognize the region Jesus was from—the Middle Eastern desert. He walked this land, a member of a people whose most consistent place of alignment and hardship had been Egypt. Moses blended in there. Mary and Joseph escaped to hide newborn Jesus there. They did not run north, into Europe, to hide. They ran south to Africa. To hide in Africa, one must be brown.

To be politically black is to occupy that rung on the ladder of human hierarchy reserved for those at the bottom. Blackness is a political construct, not of God, but of colonizing empire. Blackness was crafted in direct opposition to whiteness. If whiteness granted rights, liberties, and freedom, then blackness bestowed the opposite—confinement, control, and enslavement. If whiteness protected the image of God in one, then blackness obliterated it. To be black under colonial law was to be a thing—not a human being at all. Granted, blackness is a modern construct, crafted and perfected in the colonial era in the context of the slave trade. That said, it is not hard to see the parallels of blackness with Jesus' state of being. He was a brown man whose people had been subjugated by Rome, an explicitly white supremacist empire, for hundreds of years. His was a serially enslaved people. As residents of Nazareth—the backwater of the backwater—his was a people on the bottom of the bottom.

I am Black, Megan is white. Both of us lived her white evangelical upbringing. Both of us have come to see and know a Jesus who is miles from the white Jesus we were introduced to in white spaces.

In these pages, Megan shares her story and invites others to meet Jesus anew. She invites those disillusioned by a white Jesus to be born again, again. It changes everything.

—Lisa Sharon Harper,
author of *The Very Good Gospel*

1

HOW I "GOT SAVED"

I was four years old the first time I got saved. At least, that's what my mom tells me. I don't remember the event, but the story goes that I prayed "the sinner's prayer" and added my name to the Lamb's book of life before I could add 2 + 2.

As I got older, though, I became fairly certain that my salvation hadn't stuck. Every Wednesday night when the children's minister at my church would share from the Bible and invite us to give our lives to Christ, I felt a sinking feeling in my stomach. "If you were to die tonight, where would you spend eternity?" our minister would ask the room of wide-eyed elementary-age children. "If you leave this room and get into a car accident, would you go to heaven or hell?" I was only in kindergarten, and even waiting for lunchtime to roll around felt like an eternity. How could I possibly be confident about the eternal destination of my soul?

I grappled with doubts about my salvation throughout my childhood, waking up panicked some nights after dreaming of hellish visions, terrified that God had decided I was not truly repentant enough. So when I was twelve I got saved again. This time I remember everything about the moment. It was during another Wednesday night altar call at my church. The speaker that night invited kids who wanted to "accept Jesus as their personal Lord and Savior" to raise their hands first, then invited kids who wanted to "rededicate their lives to God" to join them. I was too embarrassed to raise my hand in the first group. After all, I had perfect Sunday school attendance and had memorized more Bible verses than anyone else in my age group. I was a model Christian kid for all intents and purposes. But I knew that our children's ministry leaders didn't know *the real me*—the me who wrestled with doubts at night, who was mean to her brothers, who could not manage to keep up with the image of the "gentle and quiet" ideal Christian young woman, and so probably wasn't saved.

I told God that I would raise my hand for rededication but would pray the first prayer—the same "sinner's prayer" my mom told me I had prayed eight years earlier. "Dear Jesus, I admit that I am a sinner. I believe that you died on the cross to be my personal Lord and Savior. Please forgive me of my sins and come into my heart. Amen."

This time, I *felt* saved. All the things the children's minister and volunteers talked about—the rushing joy, the excitement about God, the need to tell people about how good God is—I felt all of it! I definitely felt saved now, and that feeling mostly stuck with me throughout the rest of my adolescence. I was faithfully present at church, youth group, small group, and any other occasion when the church doors were open.

In high school I decided to step up my commitment to Christ. I became convinced that my desires for material things were impeding my personal relationship with God. Certain that my wish list of the latest fashions was crowding out Jesus in my heart, I committed that, except for a new Easter dress, I would not buy any new clothes that Lent. My youth leaders thought the choice was admirable, and I was lauded for my dedication. Other students were encouraged to give up possessions or habits as well.

We were urged to defend the gospel by whatever means necessary for the preservation of our souls, and the soul of our nation. Our Christian way of life was under threat, or so the Christian leaders in our community told me. I attended an apologetics class when I was sixteen, and the teacher warned us of the impending perils of college life, where we would need to defend our faith against atheists and communists. He spoke of Karl Marx's *Communist Manifesto* as if the book were Satan incarnate. I'd never heard of the book, nor had many of the non-Christians I knew, but I was ready to stand my ground. I had been warned that no educational institution—not even a Baptist college—was safe from the deceptions of academic culture. I went off to a Christian college fully prepared to defend my faith and contend for the gospel.

I took a job working in an after-school program at a faith-based nonprofit just off campus my freshman year, and that's when the trouble began. Many of the kids in the program lived in government-subsidized housing less than five minutes away from my private Christian college. Most of them were from single-parent households. A few didn't have running water or electricity in their homes. One group of siblings lived with their grandmother and didn't know their parents' whereabouts. I helped with math homework and reading proficiency and pretended that I could keep up with them in the basketball gym. Together, we read stories from the Bible. I told them about

Jesus, who loved them but hated their sin and invited them to get saved.

But the Jesus I invited them to ask into their hearts had nothing to say about the daily struggles of their families and communities. This Jesus had nothing to say about why all the businesses had fled from their neighborhood, or why Jesus cared about their souls but not about whether they had anything to eat that morning. I didn't have answers for their questions, nor for the questions welling up in my own mind as I continued to work with them. My faith was too brittle to tolerate the doubts their questions raised, so I quit.

My life didn't go back to normal, though. In one of my classes, I learned that if every member of the American church were to tithe, there would be enough money not only to provide for the hungry kids in the after-school program, but also to feed all the impoverished people in our country.[1] I would like to think I was righteously indignant in the wake of this revelation, but in reality there was probably much more weight to my indignation than my righteousness. The questions that first sparked during my freshman year took on a life of their own; they were fruitful and multiplied.

I threw myself wholeheartedly into every Christian activity on campus. I started leading a campus Bible study; I joined the Fellowship of Christian Athletes leadership team; I played guitar in one of the campus worship bands; I attended one church on Sunday morning, a different church on Sunday night, and a Bible study on Wednesday. I was determined to shore up my faith to ensure that doubt couldn't pull me away from God. But God seemed silent, and the more I tried to run from my questions, the more my questions haunted me.

I went home for Christmas my sophomore year, and despite all my attempts to study the right Scriptures and participate in the right Christian groups, I found that I barely knew how to begin to pray. My faith in God had come to rest entirely on my Christian activities and my ability to appear to be a "good Christian." For all the talk about how Christianity was "not a religion but a relationship," I no longer felt any inkling of connection with God. I didn't have a secret party-girl life I needed to repent of, as the chapel speakers often entreated us to do at Wednesday morning college chapels, and I didn't have any skeletons of terrible past sins hiding in my closet. My closet was empty, and my identity depleted. I had done all the right things, though, all the actions and disciplines that promised to bring me closer to God, but it was as if the door of salvation I had flung wide in my youth had slammed shut, and I didn't have the key to get back inside. The hours of studying and blasting worship music in my dorm and my car weren't working. "God . . . I don't even know if you're there," I barely whispered in my bedroom in the basement of my parents' house. "Help."

My dad had always emphasized that I was not the center of the universe—he even drew a picture of this reality on graph paper when I was ten. As God was silent, I fell back on what Dad had taught me, and I actively tried to stop being the center of my own life. I started volunteering again as a tutor at the nonprofit I had run away from the year prior. I needed to make sense of life and the faith that was failing me, the faith that had sounded like such good news to me at one point, but that I could see was no "gospel" for these kids, and was increasingly sounding less good to me, too.

A new president was installed at my college during my junior year. His first address to the student body was a sermon on Micah 6:8—a part of the Bible I did *not* manage to memorize as a child. "And what does God require of you? But to act justly, love mercy and walk humbly with your God."

Suddenly, everything made sense. Justice! Of course! That's what I needed to add to my gospel. I felt like I had gotten saved all over again. I bought a pair of Toms shoes, started drinking fair trade coffee (and was *very* vocal about the switch), wore peace sign earrings every day, and began sponsoring a child through a relief agency. When homecoming weekend rolled around, I planned a benefit dinner amid the festivities to raise money for the organization Invisible Children. If we were going to get together and party, I remember thinking, we might as well contribute to rescuing child soldiers while doing so. (Understandably, I stopped getting invited to as many parties after this.)

I spent the summer between my final years of college working with Campus Crusade for Christ, an evangelistic college ministry, in Santa Cruz, California. I was ready to spread the gospel, complete with the new justice upgrade! Our team leaders gave us each a stack of small blue books. The cover of the booklet announced, "Good news!" but the first page condemned the reader as a hopelessly depraved, hell-bound sinner. Not to worry, though—if the reader persevered, there was a prayer on the final page that would magically undo their depraved sinner status and secure their eternal reward in heaven with God. "Ask the people who walk past you on the sidewalk if they want to have a conversation about what really matters," the ministry leaders instructed.

We faithfully walked the streets downtown, amid restaurants and coffee shops, and stationed ourselves across the street from Anthropologie and Urban Outfitters. People had come downtown to pick up pizza for dinner or buy T-shirts from the Gap. And we stood on the corner hawking Jesus, so certain that they had room in their life for him too. Standing in this center of consumption, balancing a Frappuccino in one hand and a little blue book in the other, we invited people to stop and consume a savior on their way to get a Froyo.

Our colony of collegiate missionaries, dropped into a motel by the Pacific Ocean for the summer, had come in the name of Jesus, but not the Jesus who opened his ministry by proclaiming "good news for the poor." Nor were we able to fulfill the great commission we held in such regard. We couldn't make disciples in only six weeks' time, but we could make sure people prayed the prayer that we believed would allow them to avoid hell.

So I stood on a corner of the sidewalk in downtown Santa Cruz and asked strangers if they wanted to talk. Most did not, and the few who did were rather offended when I opened the conversation by telling them how sinful they were.

Several of those who did want to talk with me were people experiencing homelessness. They would strike up conversation as we shared street corners, and I was intrigued by what they had to say, and grateful for someone to talk to. I would sit and talk with Bonnie and Andrea over cups of coffee, listening to their stories about their lives and how they ended up without access to secure housing. We went from catching up on the corners at random to agreeing on times to meet up by the wharf to talk.

That is, until I was told by our team leaders not to talk to *those* people about what really matters. It wasn't safe, the leadership insisted. And while we were instructed to invite the people who had talked with us to join us for dinner in our compound sometime, we were not to invite anyone who was without a home or access to dinner themselves.

On the rare nights when someone did pray the prayer printed in the back of our little blue books, we would quietly shoot each other looks brimming with excitement as the new

convert walked away. We were doing it! Spreading the kingdom! We stopped at Starbucks for iced coffees to celebrate and
went on to try to strike up another life-changing conversation
with the next person who would make eye contact with us—
unless that person was asking for cash or food to get them
through the day.

After college, still chasing Jesus and justice, I took a job at
a church plant in Milwaukee, Wisconsin, and moved into a
duplex with two other people from the church. My spouse and
I moved into the lower level of the duplex, and two single guys
lived in the upper. We committed to listening to our neighbors,
drew with sidewalk chalk with the kids on the block, and
prayed for God's presence to fall afresh on our neighborhood.

I was on fire and ready to do justice all over Milwaukee. As
I listened to my neighbors, though, I learned that no one cared
about my Toms or my peace sign earrings. The lead pastor of
the church assigned readings like *The New Jim Crow* and *The
Prophetic Imagination*. These books—the first on the ways
race has warped our court system, the second on how capitalism has distorted our churches—started to help me see that
justice was a system, not a product. Justice wasn't a helpful
and hip addition to the gospel; it was intrinsic to the gospel. I
got saved again, although I wouldn't know it until years later.

I became more vocal about what I was learning from
my neighbors about access (or lack thereof) to services and
systems, about racial profiling, and economic inequality. I
started blogging and posting my reflections on social media.
Increasingly, concerned messages from friends and family
members flowed into my mailbox. Friends I'd grown up with
and leaders from my congregation back home were proud of
the "missions" work I was doing among the poor but were
concerned about the "political" nature of my recent updates.

(Ironically, I had sworn off voting for elected officials during that time.) I was gaining a whole new understanding of a world I'd lived in my entire life, and it became increasingly clear that the assumption back home was that I had lost my soul in the process.

As I write this, it has been nearly a decade since that last revelation, and once again I find my faith and my understanding of God shifting. I'm learning that the faith I love so much, that has raised me and held me tenderly, has been a crushing fist of oppression in the lives of others. I'm learning that the community of people who have given me a sense of identity for my whole life, and who encouraged me to place Christ first, have largely traded following a poor carpenter turned itinerant rabbi for pursuit of mansions in the sky. Increasingly, I am aware that the God about whom the Scripture bears witness has little to do with the god promoted in those little blue books I handed out long ago. God is shaking and reforming and reshaping my whole life all over again. This time, though, I don't think I'll be "getting" saved.

Instead, I am coming to understand salvation as a people to which I belong and a practice to which I submit. I am learning to live in ways that are consistent with the profound truth that the first opinion God has of us is not that we're terrible, rotten sinners, but that we're beloved.[2] I am no longer focused on manipulating a divine system for my own interests—eternal or otherwise. Instead, I am learning to follow in the steps of Jesus, redirecting my power and relinquishing my privilege and finding a new way of life—a life more abundant. I'm learning that there's nothing about salvation to "get," and that the whole thing is a matter of giving.

It is my hope and prayer that this book serves as a springboard for some of you, a place to begin asking questions or expanding the scope of questions you're already asking. For others, I hope this book can be a jackhammer for you, helping you dig deeper through the well-hardened places in your life that are no longer serving you (or your neighbor) well. If you don't like this book, I hope it serves as a good doorstop or fire starter.

Each chapter begins by looking back at the formation of the evangelical movement in the United States. If we're going to write a new story, it's helpful to know how we received the story we have now. I hope that telling this story will also help us identify some of the pitfalls our predecessors made along the way so we can avoid repeating them. Looking at the history of evangelicalism in the United States can also help us identify which beliefs have a deep and rich grounding in Scripture and tradition and which ones are primarily shaped by American cultural values.

After tracing some history, I'll reflect on what the Bible "says" about the matter at hand. (Spoiler: the Bible is rarely clear, but it does invite us to wrestle in some profound ways.) And then I'll explore some practical steps we can take to live into this new story, in personal and corporate ways. I ask that you, dear reader, take special care with those sections of the book. It is far too easy for us to unconsciously devour information, because we "should," without taking the time to consider how it will affect our lives moving forward. I am utterly persuaded that if we claim to have good ideas or beliefs, but don't do anything practical in the world or in our daily lives, then they're not very good ideas or beliefs. Conversely, if we are doing tons of stuff but are not thoughtful or aware of or open to the correction that another person's story offers, then we aren't really doing the best work. Orthodoxy—right beliefs—requires orthopraxy—right practices, or living, and vice versa.

Finally, I've invited some friends to share their thoughts as well. You'll find their words throughout the book. Our stories matter for our faith. The story of salvation I am living today is shaped by the stories I've been handed since childhood, the stories I've relinquished over the years, and the stories I've found more expansive than I imagined they could be along the way. The story of salvation I'm living today continues evolving as others entrust me with their own stories. As Moana's grandmother teaches us in the 2016 Disney film, "the people you love will change you." When Christ commands us to love our neighbors and our enemies, this means we're destined for lots of change. Let's shift the story together.

2

YOU'RE INVITED
Reimagining Personal Salvation

Every Sunday a handful of people gather in Milwaukee to sing and pray, break bread and share grape juice, read Scripture aloud and talk about what we like about it, what is comforting, or what makes us mad. There are people from backgrounds similar to mine, steeped in white evangelical subculture, and there are people with backgrounds I cannot even begin to imagine. People from Black Baptist churches and Quaker communities. A former Catholic nun and people who were once employed by a megachurch. People with terminal degrees and people who did not finish high school. High school students who don't use email because it's too outdated, and elders who don't use email because it doesn't make sense to them. Life in this community is tenuous and hard and beautiful and weird.

A shared commitment to a handful of behaviors governs our assembling. Practices like listening well, choosing curiosity over fear, and owning our own mistakes and missteps. These can all be summarized in one phrase: *We choose connection over consumption.*

The congregational landscape today is often characterized by the inverse: consumption over connection. Many American churches reflect a belief that the church exists primarily to meet the needs of members, rather than seeing itself as a community where lives are transformed through relationships. This impulse within the church is made evident by pastors and leaders who, in the face of accusations of wrongdoing, manipulate their congregations in order to maintain power. Congregants live into this system of acquisition when they search endlessly for what the church can do or can provide for them, or by breaking fellowship when they are "not being fed" or when expanding the table threatens their privilege.

To subvert the powerful draw of consumption, our community in Milwaukee intentionally centers its attention on Christ, trusting that by the power of the Holy Spirit every person can serve as a representation of Christ. When the youth are preparing visual and performance art pieces, our community shifts to focus on them, seeing Christ in their creative endeavors. When a congregant is ill or in need, our attention turns toward that person, seeing Christ in those who are sick or in need. When an officer-involved shooting splashes into the headlines yet again, we shift to intentionally grieve both the loss of life and the system of white supremacy that says Black lives do not bear the image of God and thus don't matter. One of the ways we talk about this way of being together is to say, "It's not your birthday . . . but it may be someone else's." This is our way of reminding each other that if one of us doesn't feel centered or celebrated, it may be because it's someone else's turn. But our day will come too.

This is a difficult way of gathering. I have to trust that as I seek connection with another person, they'll respond in kind and choose connection over consumption as well. If they don't, I'll likely be hurt. The niceness I've been taught to expect from Christians must be sacrificed for the sake of healthy, bold conflict so that we can learn to share life and resources mutually. There are awkward conversations, open discussions of boundaries, and lots of apologizing and learning to live together in better ways. The rules have not been prewritten for us, and the behaviors required by this kind of community push us up against the way most of us have been taught to act—perhaps especially in church.

As we seek to embrace the story of mutuality and connection, it is helpful first to look at the formation of the white evangelical church in America so we can identify the ways we've been malformed by it. It's a story shaped by practices of consumption and domination, a story that offers selective liberation to pacify some of its participants. Selective liberation promises grace and freedom for all, but there's a hidden asterisk, and the list of exceptions is long and varied. "Nothing can separate you from the love of God!" writes Paul in his letter to the Roman church (see Romans 8:38-39). "Yes, but your gender, race, poverty, lack of education, disability, singleness, childlessness, and so on mean God must hold you at arm's length," echoes the lie of selective liberation.

PERSONAL SALVATION

I encountered this invitation to selective liberation regularly and early. "If you can't tell me the day and the hour you gave your life to Christ, would you raise your hand? Pray this prayer with me and be sure of your salvation." The words of itinerant preachers from throughout the Great Awakenings and Billy Graham's crusades were recycled weekly in my Sunday school classroom. Every time, the question induced a deep sense of fear and anxiety in me. Although my mom had told me the story, I couldn't remember the day or the hour I gave my life to Christ or any of the particulars.

I didn't have a radical story of life change for my fellow Christians to celebrate, or to attract outsiders. During my college stint in Campus Crusade, my lack of a dramatic conversion story left me with the shame of a schoolkid wearing off-brand sneakers. One of our evangelism tactics was to share our testimonies, bearing witness to how Christ had changed our lives. My childhood was a remarkably boring joyride on the highway opposite of hell. I had no secret addictions to celebrate deliverance from; no ex-boyfriends with whom I had "gone too far." I'd never even cheated on a test. In a movement that valued purity and holiness, I was top-notch, but when the focus turned to radical conversion stories, I was off the chart on the other end.

I'm not unique in this way. I am one of a generation of people who spent their formative years relentlessly chasing the moniker "on fire" for the Lord. For most Christians who grew up in church during the post–Billy Graham era, the idea of knowing Jesus as your "personal Lord and Savior" is familiar. Most of us came into the faith before graduating high school through some knowledge of our need to admit we are sinners, believing in Jesus, and inviting him to come into our hearts as Lord.

This super-personal, highly privatized way of understanding what it means to be saved doesn't have much historical precedent, though. Conversionism, as we know it today, was an unthinkable theological position not so long ago. The church, meaning the global assembling of people around Christ throughout history, has a long (and messy) history of extending salvation to people, but there was no mention of Jesus coming to live "in people's hearts" until very recently. It is not that understanding salvation as personal is *wrong*, but an overemphasis on Jesus as *personal* Lord and Savior leaves us with an understanding of salvation that is incomplete, distorting both our view of the world and the practice of faith.

THE STORY THAT FORMS US

How we came to understand what salvation means and the way one is saved could be told as one giant story of shifts in theology and history. Christianity at its best is, and has always been, a deeply public faith. Often, major shifts in U.S. history have been immediately proceeded or followed by significant shifts in Christian theology. Christian faith affects not only the individual life of the believer, but that of the believer's community as well. To understand evangelicalism in the United States as we know it today, with its focus on the future of our eternal souls and its propensity for culture wars, it is helpful to look back for where things went off track. In fact, we must look back to before the religious right, before Billy Graham, before all the notorious and notable leaders of today. This story has its roots in the spiritual fervor that arose around the time the land we now know as the United States was being colonized.

The United States was founded in a crucible of change. When European colonizers began to arrive, the dust had settled a bit from the Protestant Reformation and ensuing Wars of Religion that ravaged Europe in the sixteenth century, and these fledgling Protestant movements were finding their own way in the broader landscape of the world.[1] The land that

Indigenous people referred to as Turtle Island (and that Europeans would rename America) seemed to the colonizers like the perfect place to test out new ideas about God and the place of religious life in society.

The narrative about what drove early colonizers to this land commonly centers on the quest for religious freedom. But their motives were far more complex than our high school history books made them out to be. Certainly, religion was important to many of these early colonizers, but their proud expressions of Protestantism led them to seek anything *but* religious tolerance. In fact, toleration of religious dissenters was achieved only when it was *demanded* by the monarchs back home, who were concerned about the poor civil and economic impact that would result from colonizers killing and exiling one another over differences in religious beliefs.[2] No matter the colonizers' intentions, their "holy experiments" ended up glorifying the same god as did the societies of their homelands—the god of acquisition and wealth—rather than providing a new way of living out the kingdom of God.

As Protestants, most early colonizers adhered to some degree to the Reformation belief in *sola scriptura*—looking to the Bible as the sole authority for formulating morality and theology. In Europe, Protestant Reformers established themselves in strong denominational camps based on their respective theologies. But in the colonies, while denominations persisted, their influence was less pronounced. In the minds of early colonizers, the word of God was made plain through the text. Participation in a congregation of some sort was valued by many, but their congregations were often no longer places of communal discernment. As a result, the implications of the interpretation of the text on a person's neighbor no longer had to be witnessed in profoundly personal ways.[3]

The rise of itinerant preachers in early America launched the Reformation value of individual interpretation of Scripture into hyperdrive, removing the reading and interpretation of Scripture from a community context and entrusting one authoritative figure who transcended all institutions to receive the word of the Lord. This move was not only a structural one that affected decisions about who could preach on Sunday morning and whether traveling ministers were expected to have anything of value to offer the community. It was also theological,[4] changing expectations about who could speak for God and how a community could recognize that the speaker had been called by God.

Increasingly, the metric of spiritual success became the ability of preachers to draw a crowd and compel large numbers of people to follow them. The theology of the itinerant preachers of the First Great Awakening would lead the colonies into not only a theological but also a political revolution,[5] and would *spiritually* form colonizers and revolutionaries into supportive citizens of the nation being wrought on the shores of Turtle Island. These colonizers began to see it as their Christian duty not just to participate. They also began to see it as their Christian duty to uphold, fight, and die for the cause of the newly formed nation and to acquire wealth and power on behalf of that nation, rather than give their lives for their neighbor or their enemy as Christ calls us to do.

Rather than a transcendent God on high who reigns absolutely over the world, colonial Christians began to envision God as more relational and personal. As they rebelled against the monarchs of the colonizing nations and ignored or flagrantly disregarded the sovereignty of the Indigenous tribes already inhabiting Turtle Island, their imagination of the kingdom of God and of God as ruler over all things faded.[6] This story has most often been told as a story about the altruistic and self-sacrificial founding fathers casting off the tyrannical, colonizing monarchy on the other side of the ocean. But even as the colonizers fought against the exploitative practices of their European monarchs, tossing tea in the ocean and assembling militias, their thirst for equity did not extend to the indentured and enslaved people whose labor was amassing the wealth on which the United States would be built. The colonialists fought for their own liberation but refused to grant the same freedom to those whose labor enriched them. This story of selective liberation, a liberation that disguised the sustained exploitation of others, would not only animate the revolution that catalyzed the birth of this nation, but also be carried forward throughout the history of the United States and shape the congregations cropping up on its shores.

This story demonstrates how a highly personalized, overtly spiritual faith can be readily manipulated by those who are powerful and difficult to challenge. It is a faith that allowed colonizers to rebel against a monarchy for being exploitative while at the same time enslaving their neighbors or stealing their neighbor's land. It is a faith that allowed evangelicals in the 1930s to feel concern for their starving neighbors during the Great Depression yet vote against policies that would help provide access to food. Such faith, the author of James would say, is dead (James 2:26).

ARENA FOLKS

In the beginning of her book *Daring Greatly*, psychologist Brené Brown, writing about the power of vulnerability and the importance of showing up for one's life, quotes Theodore Roosevelt:

It is not the critic who counts; not the man who points out how the strong man stumbles, or where the doer of deeds could have done them better. The credit belongs to the man who is actually in the arena, whose face is marred by dust and sweat and blood; who strives valiantly; who errs, who comes short again and again, because there is no effort without error and shortcoming; but who does actually strive to do the deeds; who knows great enthusiasms, the great devotions; who spends himself in a worthy cause; who at the best knows in the end the triumph of high achievement, and who at the worst, if he fails, at least fails while daring greatly.[7]

Being a people who choose connection over consumption means we become one another's "arena folks," choosing to commit to struggling together to become who God has called us to be—as individuals and as a gathered community. This work is not easy, though. Choosing to become one another's "arena folks" means that we must learn to trust the critique and correction and the blessing and the encouragement of those who are by our side in the struggle. There will be plenty of spectators who criticize or praise, but it's the feedback of those in the arena that counts. That is why it's imperative for communities to hold together both critique and care. Communities that value mutual care but ignore important voices of critique or dissent become self-congratulatory and risk an overinflated view of self. And communities that only critique and criticize and fail to provide mutual care will tear themselves apart.

I saw this approach modeled best during a theology conference in 2018. The conference was focused on the intersections of justice and the church, and organizers gathered attendees from across many social locations. Anticipating the challenges of gathering a diverse community, conference

organizers provided spaces for underrepresented and historically oppressed communities to meet autonomously during the
conference. This wasn't a new idea to me; most conferences I
had attended at that point had offered some sort of autonomous space specifically for women, people of color, women
of color, or LGBTQ people. But at this conference, during the
final session, the organizers invited participants from each of
the autonomous groups to present a report about how they,
as a group, had experienced the conference. Organizers then
took these reports with them for follow-up (as needed) and to
shape their future planning.

In my own congregation we set aside time in the worship
service each week when everyone is invited to share thoughts
or questions about the Scripture or the sermon. Without fail,
a teenage boy raises his hand to share almost every week. His
questions are always pointed and challenge the depths of my
knowledge of the text. "If God is good, why did that terrible
thing in the Scripture happen?" Not exactly a question I can
address off-the-cuff in two minutes or less. But I'm thank-
ful for his voice and his questions. Our community is better
because he gives voice to the doubt so many of us wrestle with
in the quiet of our own hearts.

What would happen if our faith communities and church
congregations adopted the same practice of pausing to listen
to how our actions affect—intentionally or not—those whose
lives are devalued by society at large? Those whose racial,
sexual, or gender identity has barred them from the doors
of so many congregations? Those whose education level or
lack of financial resources has made them seem lesser? Those
whose disability has been seen as a liability? Those whose age
has made them too young to be considered wise or too old to
be considered relevant? What if we choose to connect with,

rather than consume, one another? We might actually stand a chance at becoming the body of Christ we claim to be.

When Jesus called his disciples, he pulled a group of people together who otherwise had no business knowing one another. The community he gathered included tax collectors who were entrenched in upholding the system, Zealots who wanted to burn it all down, fishermen who had been told their formal education was finished at age thirteen and sent home to learn the family trade. The conversation around the dinner table had to be something else. Beyond the twelve closest to him, Jesus was constantly eating with the Pharisees—those seeking to preserve the best of the Jewish faith under the pressure of empire—and then turning around to go eat with someone like Zacchaeus, a tax collector helping the empire keep up the pressure. Jesus ate with the women who were shut out of the economic systems and who had no agency of their own, and with the admired and respected leaders of the community.

Just when we think we've pegged down the type of folks Jesus loves most, he turns around to accept the invitation of someone who is exactly the opposite. Because that's who Jesus loves the most—the person you can't stand, and also you. There are no clean lines, no tidy answers. No easy paths forward. The table will feel cramped and we will be unsure if another chair will fit when we pull it up to make room. But that's why we call this "good news." Anything good is worth fighting for, and anything good will be complicated enough that we will need to fight for it.

To begin to understand how to become "arena folks" for one another, we will need to shift the conversation about what it means to be "saved" in the first place. Our definitions of being a Christian will need to become broader than just those who have privately asked Jesus to come into their heart. Our

faith, if it is to be something other than a trinket to ease our
anxieties about life, must affect our embodied life together
and the ways we seek to organize our common, or public, life.
The particularities of our personhood and our faith matter,
and they must also reach beyond our personal life with the
Lord. Being part of the kingdom of God demands more of our
lives than fifteen minutes of quiet time in the private of our
own homes. We turn our attention to this expanded view of
salvation in the next chapter.

3

CONNECTION OVER CONSUMPTION
Expanding Our View of Salvation

Jim Wallis, notable Christian writer and activist, writes, "God is personal, but never private."[1] The story of salvation that many of us received, though, is one of a private faith. So it's important that we begin to ask, When does our salvation begin to affect how we engage with the world around us? When does our salvation begin to extend toward our neighbors, or our enemies? What does it look like, in the mundane and day-to-day, to transcend our own individual lives to work out this odd reality of being the body of Christ together?

Personal salvation *does* matter. In the Gospels, Jesus time and time again calls not only the twelve disciples in their differences and particularities, but also characters like Zacchaeus and the Samaritan woman at the well. God certainly is concerned with our particularity, and the ways in which we encounter the initial call of salvation vary. For Zacchaeus, salvation comes to his house after the wealthy and exploitative tax collector repays the money he has extorted from his community (Luke 19:1-10). For the woman at the well, salvation is extended in the breaking down of social expectations as Jesus asks her for a drink (John 4:1-42). Hagar, in her desperation, declares, "You are the God who sees me" (Genesis 16:13). Elijah is sent to the widow of Zarephath, and her oil jar never runs dry (1 Kings 17:7-16). Philip is sent to the eunuch from Ethiopia as he puzzles over the words of the prophet (Acts 8:26-40).

The particularities of our personhood are not lost on God, and the love of God necessitates that our engagement be freely chosen. This choosing, though, is not the selective liberation of Great Awakening firebrands and evangelistic crusaders. It is more like deciding to pull up a seat to a raucous dinner party table or choosing to run out your front door when your childhood friends come knocking with an invitation to join their game. Theologian Julie Canlis describes it this way: "The Spirit says to each one of us, 'Okay, who's in?'"[2]

There is a personal aspect to salvation, but this becomes restrictive and reductive when we insist on experiencing salvation *only* in the particularities of our personhood. "Persons are imperfect if self-centered or solitary individuals," writes theologian Catherine Mowry LaCugna. "Perfection for all persons, divine or human, resides in loving and knowing another, . . . being who one is in relation to another."[3]

I will leave the dinner party hungry if I don't pull up a chair and take part in the meal, and I am no fun as a fellow guest at the table if I am only concerned with stuffing my face. Similarly, I will miss out on the game if I only stand at the window and watch my friends play, but if I insist on always being team captain, my friends won't enjoy the game. Choosing to jump in personally is necessary for the full enjoyment of these experiences, but remembering that salvation is more than a personal event is equally necessary for full participation in the work of salvation.

When we decide to run out the front door and join the game or to pull up a chair to the table, there are different aspects of how we relate to God, our neighbors, and the systems of this world that we will need to unlearn or let go of so we can more clearly hear the voice of Love calling us onward. None of us reads the Bible with completely clear eyes, and none of us is able to check our identity and experiences at the door when doing theology. The question is not, "Will our theology be contextual?" but, "Will we be aware enough of our context to account for it as we do theology?" Presenting theology without being aware of, or while being dishonest about, how our context and experience inform our theology is a hallmark of a consumeristic framework. This way of doing theology functions as a damning sort of baptism, sanctifying any viewpoint put forward by a person of privilege as inherently, objectively correct and worthy of universal application. Anyone who disagrees with this kind of viewpoint is deemed incorrect and archaic, and is seen as someone who should be either corrected or cut off.[4]

There is a double edge to the overemphasis on personal salvation: on the one hand it is unbearably heavy, and on the other it is so weak it has proven almost worthless. An exclusively personal view of salvation creates an understanding of salvation that depends completely on the spiritual performance of each individual in isolation. If you are struggling, or discouraged, or overwhelmed, perhaps you should pray more? How *is* your *personal relationship* with the Lord? This view of salvation places an enormous burden on the shoulders of a solitary human being, and is far from the light burden that Jesus described. I've heard more than one pastor quip from the pulpit, "If God feels far away, guess who moved?"—implying that those who are questioning or suffering must be far from God's presence and have no one to blame but themselves. This could not be further from the witness of Scripture, which time and again bears witness to a God who is *with* us—Emmanuel.

An overly personalized view of salvation also creates an understanding of salvation that lacks the strength to address systemic suffering. This failure is easily observed in historical instances like the inaction of white evangelicals during the civil rights movement (certainly in the 1950s and '60s, but this still persists with regard to anti-racist work today). The "soul saving" view of personal salvation preached by evangelicals of that era produced "sentiment and possibly even anguish about the plight of oppressed people, but it [was] not adequately equipped to do much more than lament and mourn the plight of 'those people.'"[5] When salvation is a strictly personal, spiritual business between an individual and God, it lacks muscle sufficient for standing up against the systemic suffering of humanity.

It is far easier to tell a vibrant and compelling story about being converted and experiencing Jesus living "in your heart" than it is to pick up your cross and follow Christ in working against systemic suffering. If Jesus lives in your heart, he is close enough to comfort and guide, but small enough that he doesn't really mess anything up. If Jesus is in my heart, he can be in there for a long time convicting and purifying me but never touching the way I treat my neighbor, the way I manage my finances, or the way I vote. If my relationship with Jesus is merely a label for a deeply felt, but purely private, religious faith,[6] then I can spend my whole life investing in building a kingdom without ever considering if I'm supporting the kingdom of God or an empire of this world.

PEOPLE OF GOD

If we enter salvation through a personal experience of God's grace and love, then the imperative next question is, *Into what are we entering?* If we enter into a personal relationship with God but stop there, we experience the theological equivalent of visiting someone's home but refusing to go any further than standing in the doorway and insisting that the way we enter is in fact the whole thing.

For the first three-quarters of Western church history, and more than that outside the Western context, salvation was not a private matter worked out in a person's heart. Rather, it was conceived of as a communal state. Joining the church was synonymous with becoming part of the family or the people of God, continuing to build on the covenants made with Israel in the Hebrew Bible.

Primarily, the call of salvation is a declaration of belonging. For the Israelites, the call was to return and to remember their belonging in the covenant God had made with their ancestors. This call then was carried forward to the church in the Christian Scriptures. As Paul writes in Romans 4 and Galatians 3, the covenant made to Abraham is extended to all now, in Christ, by faith.

Humans are told every day in a million ways that we are deficient in some way—that we lack the job, the hair, or the relationship we need to be happy and whole. The promise of salvation stands in stark contrast to this. The message of God to humanity is first of all a declaration of blessing and goodness. Before anything else, we are loved.[7]

But this love is not intended to be a purely personal affair between just an individual and Jesus. Theologian Gordon Fee writes about salvation this way:

> Though entered individually, salvation is seldom if ever thought of simply as a one-on-one relationship with God. While such a relationship is included, to be sure, "to be saved" means especially to be joined to the people of God. . . . God is saving *a people* for his name, not a miscellaneous, unconnected set of individuals. . . . God is not just saving individuals and preparing them for heaven; rather, he is creating *a people* among whom he can live and who in their life together will reproduce God's life and character.[8]

The Love that holds us from the beginning holds within it hope and identity, which are both inherent to the very nature of salvation. Unlike a transaction through which a person intends to obtain a product, in this understanding of salvation the person receiving salvation is welcomed home and into life. This salvation invites us into a life that is indeed more abundant.

"Linking the commandment to love God and the commandment to love one another," writes theologian Tomáš Halík, "is a way of discovering the God who 'disappeared,' and specifically, in *our relationship to our neighbor*." Being inundated with activities and devotionals in college didn't prevent God from "disappearing" in my doubts, but it wasn't by praying harder and studying more that I rediscovered God. Unlike the overly personal view of salvation endemic to the evangelical movement in the United States, in this understanding of salvation, when God seems to have "disappeared," the responsibility to find a way forward is not on the individual navigating the dark night alone. Their salvation is held with their neighbor. The "church mothers"—the wise elder African

American women on my block—say, "I'll hold your faith for you." Halík, in the same vein, insists that "God *happens* where we love people."[9]

But this move to love and be loved in community with one's neighbors is about more than just having someone to "hold your faith" when you cannot. The ethic of love "overcomes the temptation to turn God into an object."[10] The God who loves and draws us into receiving and practicing love may *not* be consumed like a product or tucked away inside one's heart like a superstitious knickknack. Love, writes Halík, "is the courage . . . to step outside oneself" and in so doing to make things one—to bring all things to complete restoration—without destroying them.[11]

PUBLIC WITNESS

However, it is possible to engage Christian faith personally and become part of a people without ever bringing our faith into the public sphere. Jim Wallis writes, "Restricting God to private space was the great heresy of the twentieth-century evangelicalism. Denying the public God is a denial of biblical faith itself, a rejection of the prophets, the apostles, and Jesus himself."[12] The God we bear witness to as Christians is a deeply public God who is intimately concerned with the common life of people.

In the book of Exodus, God upends the economic engine of one of the great empires of the world by liberating the enslaved Hebrew people from imperial Egypt. Later, the same people are carried off into exile because they, too, have failed to uphold the justice of God in their midst—the exploited have become exploiters because they have forgotten how to live as liberated people together, embodying the love and equity that honors their neighbors and those they see as "other."[13]

The gospel evangelist Mark opens his account of the life of Christ with a loaded political statement: "This is the *gospel* of Jesus Christ" (see Mark 1:1). *Gospel* was a term used by the Roman military to inform a region of their impending engraftment into the empire. Jesus himself was executed by the Roman Empire by means of crucifixion, a form of capital punishment reserved for traitors and political rabble-rousers. Ours is and has been an *inherently* public faith from the beginning.

For examples of this facet of faith, it is imperative that we turn to witnesses outside the white evangelical world for instruction. Even when white evangelicals have engaged in public witness—opposing legal access to abortion and fighting against civil rights for African Americans, and then LGBTQ people—their public witness has been selectively embodied and in ways that often violate rather than uphold the command to love neighbors and enemies. White evangelical public witness has often been led by those pursuing ideological power, not a sacrificial love that seeks the flourishing of another— even if that "other" disagrees with them. Increasingly, we are discovering that when it comes time to embody proclaimed values, white evangelical bodies find themselves in behaviors dissonant with the values their mouths would proclaim.

White evangelicals have continued to preach traditional family values, but the dissonance between values and actions has become deafening as waves of survivors of sexual abuse come forward and stories of abuse in Christian circles mount into the thousands. The dissonance has become deafening as children are separated from parents and family guardians at the southern border of the United States. White evangelicals continue to preach a value for human life, but the dissonance is deafening as innocent, unarmed Black and brown people fall in the streets. I began to learn how to embody the values

I've professed for my entire life only when I started listening to, learning from, and following the leadership of people who were not white evangelicals. I learned how to embody a value for family when my neighbors showed up with food and clothing and well-wishes for my newborn daughter, because people on the block have to look out for each other. I learned how to value life by following the lead of Black activists and pastors by gathering in the streets of my neighborhood to call for accountability when Sylville Smith was shot and killed in Milwaukee's Sherman Park neighborhood.

One of the great public witnesses in the United States was Ida B. Wells, a journalist and anti-lynching activist who lived around the turn of the twentieth century. Her faith informed and sustained her prophetic work of protesting lynching in the early 1900s—especially as a Black woman. She dismissed white Christianity in the United States as hypocritical: "The nation cannot profess Christianity, which makes the golden rule its foundation stone, and continue to deny equal opportunity for life, liberty and the pursuit of happiness to the black race."[14] Wells wrote extensively, publishing editorials and pamphlets denouncing lynching as well as other less blatantly terrorizing forms of racism. She traveled widely, taking her case against lynching across the Atlantic to Britain. Her quest to fight racialized violence was uncompromising and highly political, and stemmed unapologetically from her faith.[15]

Another public witness we would be remiss to overlook is Bayard Rustin. Rustin's mother, Julia, was an active member of her local African Methodist Episcopal church and a charter member for the NAACP. Bayard himself held to the Quaker faith of his grandmother and began his life of activism as a conscientious objector during World War II thanks to his theologically informed pacifism.[16] Rustin's most notable work of public witness was orchestrating the 1963 March on Washington, although he stayed out of the spotlight personally. As an openly gay, African American man in the 1960s, his life existed in tenuous intersections. Despite all the activists and politicians he interacted with, Rustin maintained throughout his life that it was his faith which informed and spurred his public action.[17]

Today we can look to the physical places and communities of people the U.S. government has overlooked (or systematically undermined) and see people boldly living out of a belief that there is another way. Pastor Carlos Rodríguez, in the wake of Hurricane Maria and the abysmal failure of the U.S. government to provide support for cleanup and rebuilding in Puerto Rico, relocated his family to the island. They continue to work rebuilding homes and cleaning the debris that still clings to the shores of the island.[18]

Rev. Dr. William Barber II, the force behind North Carolina's Moral Mondays movement and the now-nationwide Poor People's Campaign, has taken up the unfinished work of Martin Luther King Jr., organizing and instructing groups across the United States in the tactics of fusion politics, which brings together people of widely varying backgrounds and from different political parties as a means of standing against racism and exploitation of the poor.[19] Artist and activist Bree Newsome Bass, the woman who climbed the flagpole of the statehouse in Charleston, South Carolina, in 2015 to tear down the Confederate flag, did so while reciting the Lord's Prayer and Psalm 27.[20]

The list could go on and on (in fact, I made one for you—check out the list of recommended readings in the back of this book), but the faithful public witness of the people of God, while largely absent from the white evangelical movement, has been at work all along in the African American, Latinx, Asian American and Pacific Islander, Indigenous, and LGBTQ Christian communities. Learning to bear public witness will require white Christians to listen to and learn humbly from our siblings who have great wisdom in this regard. Christianity emerged as a religion of outsiders under persecution. The privilege afforded to white evangelicals in the United States numbs us to the power of some of the deepest truths of our faith.

The following chapters will explore ways to embody our faith in this threefold way of "personal, people, and public" as we imagine our story anew, paying particular attention to some of the volatile intersections of faith and public life today. It's challenging enough to push the bounds of our spiritual imagination under the best circumstances, but when tensions rise it's almost impossible to maintain a posture open to what God may be inviting us into as we work toward connection instead of consumption. This is the work the Holy Spirit invites us to, though, and Christ who goes before us in all things knows us in our weakness and discomfort (Hebrews 4:15).

Each chapter will look at the historical and biblical precedent for engaging in the issue at hand. I've divided each of the application sections of these chapters into practices of "unlearning and returning" the personal, people, and public aspects of embodying the Christian faith.

When it comes to the "personal" aspect of embodying faith, unlearning is critical. There is often significant work to be done in our congregations and in the broader public sphere, but we are unable to do this work well—honestly and with the ability to engage and integrate critique in a meaningful way—if we have not first done significant unlearning work.

4

THE AUTHORITIES ARE GOD'S SERVANTS

Connection over Consumption in Politics

My mother drove me to the polls the first election after my eighteenth birthday. She was as proud as she had been on the days I took my first steps and learned to read. I was crossing another major milestone. I cast my vote that day, but after that I didn't vote again for over seven years. I was disillusioned with the whole political process. From my perspective, living on campus at my private Christian college, I couldn't see any impact of politics on our daily lives. And besides, if I truly believed that Jesus was Lord and King, then did it matter if I cast a vote for a politician? Politics felt like a waste of time, and a divisive one at that.

I moved to Milwaukee when I was twenty-two, and after living in the city for a couple of years, I started to question my indictment of politics. The policies being enacted in the state capital and in the nation's capital were absolutely affecting daily life for my neighbors and me in huge ways, for better or worse. When budget decisions were made, my neighborhood was usually pretty low on the list of communities invested in. When we did crack the list, the specific investment was often misguided at best, leaving us with beautifully renovated storefronts along one of the main arteries through my neighborhood that, even a decade later, have rarely been inhabited by the businesses the city hoped to attract. When the Affordable Care Act passed, more people in my neighborhood had access to some form of health insurance, and my own coverage became more comprehensive. I began to see that politics, and my involvement in them, did matter in day-to-day life.

Increasingly, I became vocal about my perspectives on the policies coming from the state and federal legislatures. I went to meetings with local representatives about immigration reform and joined in protests when policy decisions were handed down that would harm people in my community. Sometimes people from back in my hometown would push back, asking, "Why are you talking about politics? This is a distraction from the gospel." They encouraged me to pray for my elected officials, rather than criticize them.

But prayer and prophetic critique are not mutually exclusive, and when we insist that they are, we diminish the scope and impact of our prayer. Marching with Martin Luther King Jr. in Selma, Alabama, Rabbi Abraham Joshua Heschel commented that he was praying with his feet. In a similar vein, Frederick Douglass, a formerly enslaved man, noted that he prayed for freedom for twenty years but received no answer until he started praying with his legs. Our prayers for those in authority need not necessarily be prayers of blessing, nor are they only to be uttered in the privacy of our own homes.

When we fall into thinking that politics is a purely private affair, we miss the invitation to see the kingdom of God as a reality that reorganizes our systems and power structures so that no one person, race, or class amasses more and more for themselves to the detriment and oppression of others. When politics is purely private, it becomes a trinket we can tuck inside our heart next to Jesus, a Magic 8 Ball we can consult for predetermined answers in the ballot box rather than a rubric for assessing how we might engage the world around us in ways faithful to the way of Christ.

THE STORY THAT FORMS US: BECOMING PATRIOTS

Before the two world wars, church leaders in the United States were consistently divided on whether and how to support the government. Pastors and Christian leaders were often critical of the government. Their critiques were often at least partially grounded in their belief that Jesus' second coming was imminent and so the governments and systems of this world would no longer matter. During and after the world wars, though, a rising anxiety in the United States over the possibility of traitors and communists in their midst pushed these leaders to reconsider their position. Evangelicals in the late 1940s and early 1950s who had once been critical of governmental actions became zealous supporters of the U.S. government, performing acts of patriotism to demonstrate their political allegiance.[1]

After the United States entered the First World War, white American evangelicals went to great lengths to support the effort. Moody Bible Institute began selling Liberty bonds, breaking with their founder's philosophy of discouraging corporate political action for Christians.[2] Itinerant preacher Abraham Vereide believed a "righteous 'remnant,'" whom he defined as successful, conservative Christian men from the business world, would be the ones to rid the United States of its "moral decadence" and turn the tide of the war.[3]

Increasingly, the previously distinct religious and national identities of American Christians collapsed. To be an American was to be capitalist was to be a good Christian, as opposed to an atheistic communist loyal to the Axis powers. Pastors and public faith leaders bought into the myth of the nation's Christian roots, proclaiming the benefits of free-market capitalism and warning against the woes of regulation, unions, or anything else that smacked of communism in their minds.

This synchronizing of ideals also strengthened resistance to the perceived evil of President Franklin Roosevelt's New Deal legislation. Although religious opposition to the New Deal echoed in the background during the 1930s, that opposition was far from mainstream.[4] But by the 1940s, the National Association of Manufacturers (NAM) hit on using faith as the "antidote" to "check the virus of collectivism" that they believed was plaguing their businesses with regulations, higher taxes, and a unionized workforce.[5]

NAM recruited James Fifield, a Congregationalist minister from Los Angeles whose congregants included some of Hollywood's wealthiest and most influential residents. Before World War II, Fifield had decried the New Deal, saying that "it caused Americans to covet what the wealthy possessed,"[6] and that the legislation of social welfare programs was an act of stealing, thus also in violation of the Ten Commandments. "Every Christian should oppose the totalitarian trends of the New Deal," Fifield wrote in a 1938 pamphlet. "The way out [of economic distress] for America is not ahead but back. . . . How far back? Back as far as the old Gospel which exalted individuals, which placed responsibility for thought on individuals, and which insisted that individuals should be free spirits under God."[7] Given that one of the express reasons the Ten Commandments were given to Israel was to shape their community life in equitable ways, Fifield's assertation was clearly shaped more by the interests of his congregation and NAM than by the text itself.

The election of Dwight D. Eisenhower ushered in a new era of ardently felt, yet vaguely defined, religious influence in government. Eisenhower abruptly ended Truman-era civil rights measures, claiming that racial discrimination was not a societal problem but a matter of individual feelings.[8] At the urging of Billy Graham and Abraham Vereide, Eisenhower established the National Prayer Breakfast. The first breakfast boasted the theme "Government under God," a compelling yet noncommittal name that reflected concern more with fighting communism than with promoting any particular religious doctrine. "All free government is firmly founded in a *deeply felt* religious faith," Eisenhower admonished the guests.[9]

Church attendance soared to record highs during the great "under God" awakening of the Eisenhower years, although formation for adherents to the faith seemed to be lacking. A 1950 Gallup Poll found that 80 percent of Americans believed the Bible was the "revealed word of God," but only 47 percent could name even one author of the four gospels.[10] Another poll found that most Americans believed the "most significant event in world history" was Columbus's "discovery" of Turtle Island. The birth and crucifixion of Christ tied for the fourteenth most significant event, alongside the first airplane flight.[11] The "deeply felt religious faith" of Eisenhower became the gospel truth of the era, ushering into the hearts of true believers their own personal Jesus.

From the Eisenhower era forward, white Christians, and particularly white evangelicals, became some of the most dependable supporters of the U.S. government. In the 1960s and '70s, as concerns about the spread of communism continued to run high, white evangelicals lined up to support the Vietnam War wholeheartedly. The collapsed matrix that equated American with Christian with capitalist compelled them to support the war not only on political grounds, but as a moral and religious imperative. The financial support that certain evangelical organizations enjoyed from executives of Agent Orange manufacturer DuPont perhaps factored into this support as well.[12]

Additionally, white evangelicals found themselves at odds with the African American pastors of the civil rights movement, including with Dr. King himself. King's "Beyond Vietnam" sermon openly critiqued the militarism of the United States as he admonished the nation to learn to live together, lest they perish separately.[13]

In the late 1970s the Moral Majority movement emerged, and within the first few years the organization grew to boast an annual operating budget of multiple millions of dollars.[14] The leaders of the movement called people of faith to vote for candidates who were "pro-life, pro-traditional family, pro-moral and pro-American."[15] Movement leader Jerry Falwell encouraged evangelical Christians across the United States to fulfill their threefold mission. The first two points of the mission were to get people saved and baptized, mandates that were similar to the great commission issued by Jesus at the end of Matthew's gospel (28:16-20). But the third point indicated just how far the evangelical movement had moved from their isolationist tendencies at the beginning of the century: Falwell exhorted his fellow evangelicals to ensure that these newly saved and baptized people were also registered to vote![16]

THE BIBLE SAYS . . .

For the purposes of this book, *politics* is defined as "the system by which public life and resources are organized." With this definition as the basis of our conversation, it should come as no surprise that religious practice has a *lot* to do with politics. What resources are brought as offerings, and who decides? Who gets to eat the meat from the sacrifices? What does the command to practice Sabbath say about the way public life is organized? What is it about other nations that puts them at odds with the way God calls Israel to live? The Hebrew Scriptures are full of interesting commentary about political systems, including both affirmation and critique.

Even if we restrict our investigation to the monarchy of Israel, the perspective of Scripture on political systems is, at best, a wildly mixed bag. Joseph, after being imprisoned in Egypt, assisted Pharaoh in planning and preparing for a famine, and his work ultimately provided for his family (Genesis 41–45). But in Exodus, God is adamantly opposed to Egypt's oppressive and exploitative rule and delivers the Hebrew people from its grasp (Exodus 1).

Throughout the narratives in Joshua and Judges, Israel's neighboring nations are seen as wicked and needing to be destroyed, but in the Prophets, God uses these foreign nations as the instruments of purifying Israel through exile.[17] King Nebuchadnezzar of Babylon is portrayed both as the evil king who throws those faithful to God into the fire and, later, as the penitent ruler who has turned to belief in the God of Israel. In Esther, the king of Persia nearly destroys Israel, but in the Prophets another king of Persia is granted the title "messiah" (Isaiah 45).

Although tradition considers David and Solomon to both be "good kings," it is under their reigns that Israel commits the sin which God repeatedly called them to resist: they forget that they were slaves in Egypt and force their own people into enslaved labor to build David's palace and Solomon's temple.[18]

But the chapter of the Bible most frequently referenced in discerning a Christian's role in government or politics comes from the Christian Scriptures—Romans 13. The first seven verses of the chapter provide a strong statement about respecting the governmental authorities:

> Let every person be subject to the governing authorities; for there is no authority except from God, and those authorities that exist have been instituted by God. Therefore whoever resists authority resists what God has appointed, and those who resist will incur judgment. For rulers are not a terror to good conduct, but to bad. Do you wish to have no fear of the authority? Then do what is good, and you will receive its approval; for it is God's servant for your good. But if you do what is wrong, you should be afraid, for the authority does not bear the sword in vain! It is the servant of God to execute wrath on the wrongdoer. Therefore one must be subject, not only because of wrath but also because of conscience. For the same reason you also pay taxes, for the authorities are God's servants, busy with this very thing. Pay to all what is due them—taxes to whom taxes are due, revenue to whom revenue is due, respect to whom respect is due, honor to whom honor is due.

Many Christians have interpreted this passage to mean that they are called to complete obedience to all government authorities. Yet it is neglectful to read this text as blanket support of whatever government exists. As Paul was writing these words, he was likely imprisoned *by Roman authorities*, and not for one instance alone! Tradition holds that Paul was imprisoned on multiple occasions and was ultimately executed by Rome, as were Peter and many other apostles and early

Christians. John was exiled by the empire. And Jesus' crucifixion was carried out by the governing authorities. To use Romans 13 to negate the strong biblical witness of political resistance and critique is to take the chapter completely out of its original context, leading to a reading of this letter without any degree of consistency.

UNLEARNING AND RETURNING: PERSONAL

During the summer of 2018 I took my six-year-old daughter to protest the enforcement of family separation policies outside the Immigration and Customs Enforcement office in our city. While the headlines of the crisis at the southern border had driven me to take action, the organizers of the local protest were Latinx clergy who had been protesting for months— long before national news began to take notice. They called their protest the Jericho Walk and took time to march around the ICE office seven times each week while praying. Like the Israelites so many years ago, these pastors and priests were trusting that God could make the walls of unjust policies and prison cells come tumbling down as well.

Like Abraham Heschel and Frederick Douglass, we prayed with our feet and our legs that day. I carried a banner protesting family separation, and my daughter picked wildflowers along the sidewalks outside the ICE building. The adult protestors called out the vile and broken systems endemic to society, and the children gathered up beauty and reminded us to notice the butterflies.

Politics, at its most basic level, is simply how we organize people and resources. If I assume that life in my community is organized well because all the people who are just like me appear to be flourishing, without regard for how people not like me are affected, then I risk tending only to certain parts of creation while others around me are suffering. Conversely, if I see only the suffering and anger and harm of a system organized explicitly to benefit some, to the detriment of others, then I risk missing the beauty of God's grace at work, peeking up like daisies through concrete. Prayer for the authorities, and political engagement broadly, always includes both.

There are many ways Christians can engage faithfully with politics. I believe that voting in local, state, and federal elections is one way of faithfully engaging. Some Christians choose to abstain from voting as a reflection of their conviction that no politician is ultimately our savior. While there is merit to this belief, choosing to abstain from voting is a choice afforded mainly to those whose privilege within the system insulates them from being negatively affected by changes in policy.

However, if you do not feel comfortable voting in response to your own conscience and discernment through research, conversation, and prayer, then I'd recommend that you speak with someone you know who does not have voting rights—an undocumented immigrant or someone convicted of a felony whose state does not allow them to vote—and vote for the candidates they recommend.[19]

Regardless of whether you vote, calling or writing your elected officials is a great way to stay involved in the political process. While federal legislation tends to grab our newsfeeds and headlines most of the time, it is easiest to have a large impact on a local level—as William Barber has done in organizing Moral Mondays in the state of North Carolina. Subscribe to your local newspaper, or make it a point to read a copy of it online or in the library, and look for policies and legislation being enacted locally that you would like to influence; then call, write, or request meetings with your officials to make your voice heard.

Engaging in civil disobedience is another way to engage in a personal witness to Jesus as Lord—although this often crosses into public witness as well. My friend Ben has taught me more about what it means to embody solidarity with the oppressed, and bear witness to the kingdom in this way, than almost anyone else. This is part of his story.

Civil disobedience as conformity to Christ

Ben Swihart

On Black Friday, November 27, 2015, after the release of dashcam footage of the shooting of Laquan McDonald, the city of Chicago was teetering on the edge of chaos. Old guard civil rights icons collaborated with young radicals to plan a big march down the Magnificent Mile, an upscale stretch of Michigan Avenue, on the biggest shopping day of the year. In coordination with the police, the protest-turned-parade route was cordoned off from traffic to keep the protest from completely interrupting the busiest day of the year at the temples of capital. So I walked into traffic, and man, were the cops mad about it. They acted like they had done us a favor by shepherding us through the crosswalks, but our purpose wasn't to march and be seen. It was to create a scene. Direct action isn't meant to be a virtue signal or a vanity project, it's a disruption that demands we ask the hard questions about power: Who hoards it, who is excluded from it, and who really wields it?

I never met Laquan McDonald. I never met Rekia Boyd either. But I knew them. They were both African American young people who died in my neighborhood, murdered by police officers.

When justice delayed and justice denied pushed the people of our city to the brink, we had no choice but to show up. It took four hundred days of coordinated lawsuits, activism, and protest before we were allowed a glimpse of the video from Laquan McDonald's case. We were in the streets protesting that night, and for several days after. I saw officers hitting people and shoving people with their riot gear. One of the police tactics involved jabbing us in the ribs with their billy clubs and, when we moved in response, yelling "Stop resisting!" to justify a violent escalation. I had my legs kicked and was shoved over with a bike while sitting down on the sidewalk, and I wasn't even close to the most rambunctious part of the crowd.

André Trocmé, a French pastor who led the nonviolent resistance to the Nazis in the French village of Le Chambon, said that they didn't decide to break the law, they just decided to love the neighbors who showed up at their doorstep. That's what I imagine discipleship looks like—showing up for the people in our world who are in pain, putting our bodies on the line, literally, for the sake of the flourishing of the image of God in others. It sounds like what Jesus did. What if the whole church showed up and surrounded the ICE officers trying to dismember the body of Christ and deport one of its brothers, like members of a church in North Carolina did in 2018? What if the whole church showed up to block and destroy the pipelines that are poisoning our water and destroying God's precious gift of creation, like Catholic Workers did in Des Moines in 2017? What if the whole church showed up at the border with food and water like Scott Warren did? What if the whole church brought bolt cutters to the concentration camps? What if the whole church showed up and sabotaged the weapons of war, dismantled the machinery of oppression, burned down the very superstructures that are grinding our humanity into dust? Can we imagine for a second what that catechesis of our faith would give witness to in the world?

UNLEARNING AND RETURNING: PEOPLE

If the Bible tells a complex story of how to relate to political systems, then the history and traditions of the church are even more complex. Focusing only on the witness of the evangelical church in the United States lessens the dissonance, but not by much.

At the founding of the United States, some revolutionaries resisting British colonialism saw themselves as acting within a Christian witness. White slave-owning plantation owners saw themselves as acting in harmony within the biblical witness, because Paul's letters instruct the enslaved to obey their masters. Conversely, enslaved people who formed their own expression of Christianity in the "hush harbors" on the plantation saw it as their Christian duty to resist, escape, and rebel. Leaders within the movement to abolish slavery such as Nat Turner and Sojourner Truth were also deeply informed by their faith and by the witness of Scripture.

During the civil rights movement, King, Bayard Rustin, and the organizers of the Southern Christian Leadership Conference (SCLC) primarily found their grounding in Scripture, largely drawing from the exodus narrative and the Prophets of the Hebrew Bible. For those engaged in the struggle for civil rights, churches were often ground zero for training and equipping activists in tactics of nonviolent resistance, opening the doors to their sanctuaries and fellowship halls to serve as meeting spaces.

There is no singular story of how communities of Christians have traditionally gathered to support or resist political action, but there are principles that can guide us moving forward. The witness of Christ suggests that our investment in the way our shared life is organized should be for the sake of the other, not just for our personal benefit or gain alone. This means that people like me with relative social privilege need to listen to people who are disempowered or disenfranchised by our social system in order to learn about the gaps in the system.

Simple things, like getting to know the community association affiliated with the neighborhood where your church building is located, can be ways of getting involved with the political process. Offering meeting space free of charge to the neighborhood association or a community organization is an easy way to begin listening well to the community you are rooted in.

In the 2010s, William Barber reignited the movement started decades earlier by King, the Poor People's Campaign, and began using fusion politics to organize people of faith for social change in the political arena. Barber's Moral Mondays movement in North Carolina worked to combat gerrymandering and policies harmful in terms of education, job access, and social programs in the state. Moral Monday protests drew national attention, spawning chapters of the Poor People's Campaign in states across the United States. Getting involved with your local chapter of the Poor People's Campaign is a great way to bear witness to Christ's work in the world through a gathered community.

Another way for a congregation to bear witness as the people of God is to become a sanctuary church through the New Sanctuary Movement, helping to advocate for and shelter undocumented migrants. If your congregation does not have space to serve as physical sanctuary, consider hosting a training for non-attorney volunteers to assist at immigration clinics and process paperwork for those seeking legal immigration or asylum status.

UNLEARNING AND RETURNING: PUBLIC

In some ways, because politics affects our shared life, all political engagement is public. Yet some actions have a decidedly more public feel to them. Writing letters to the editor of your local newspaper or showing up to express concerns or support at a city council meeting are a few such actions. On one occasion several years ago, about a dozen people from my congregation showed up to testify at a city council meeting about a strip club with ties to suspected human trafficking that was seeking a permit for a new club in the heart of downtown. We spoke fiercely about our concerns, and the permit was denied.

Because our public witness so often has political implications, many of the ways to unlearn our consumeristic ways and return to conformity to Christ in the political arena are outlined in the following chapters of this book. The German theologian Karl Barth is credited with advising people to read the Bible in one hand and the newspaper in the other. The ways in which we can best engage in public witness to the lordship of Christ will likely be different depending on our context, but a great place to start is by staying informed about what is going on in our communities and the ways in which our elected officials are moving us either closer to or further from the all-encompassing peace and embodied mutuality and solidarity that the kingdom of God promises.

5

WE ARE ALL ONE IN CHRIST, SEPARATELY PLEASE

Connection over Consumption in Relationships across Race

I grew up saying the U.S. Pledge of Allegiance every morning from the time I was six. My mom would gather my infant brother and me in our dining room, which transformed into a school classroom Monday through Friday, drawing our attention to the tabletop-size flag we kept for such purposes.

I pledge allegiance to the flag of the United States of America.

At that point in my life I didn't have many things memorized, but the repetition made it stick. Stand at attention, don't be silly, right hand over your heart.

One nation under God, indivisible.

I didn't know what *indivisible* meant. For most of my childhood I assumed it was similar to *invisible*—which made sense
in my young mind after the line about being a nation "under
God." God was invisible, so maybe the nation under God was
too? The only thing seared into my young consciousness with
anywhere near the same fervor as patriotism was religion. We
were churchgoing folks, devoted Christians. Sunday morning,
Sunday evening, Wednesday night kind of folks. It only made
sense that we were also proud to be Americans—our nation
was the *one nation* under God.

With liberty and justice for all.

Those words didn't make sense to me as a child either, but
I knew they meant that in this country everyone got treated
equally. Ours was a fair society; everyone had equal access. I
grew up in the coal fields of West Virginia. My family lived on
land behind my grandparents' home, which was a smaller par-
cel of land that had belonged to my great-grandparents before
them. "Liberty and justice for all" meant we had the same shot
at success and flourishing as the family fifteen minutes away in
the subdivision with country club access, and the people who
lived a two-minute walk around the bend renting a tiny plot of
land in the trailer park. Liberty and justice for all, that's what
made America so great.

I was in high school before I started to wonder if maybe
this rose-colored vision of the United States was incomplete.
My junior year, I went with our neighbor once a week to tutor
students in a disinvested neighborhood in our town. I spent my
Tuesday afternoons helping third-grade girls progress toward
reading on grade level in a small classroom that smelled like
overdone boxed macaroni and cheese. After I had been tutor-
ing there for six months, one of the girls broke down in tears
during a particularly frustrating homework session. She started

telling me about all the challenges her family was facing. She told me that her dad was in jail and that they didn't always have food to eat. She cried and cried, and I had no answers for her, other than to pray with her that her dad would get out of jail soon. I tried to ask her if she was saved, if she had invited Jesus to live in her heart, but that didn't sit right with me and I wasn't sure why.

Soon after moving to Milwaukee as an adult, one of the ceilings in the house my neighbor was renting caved in. It was the ceiling in her young child's bedroom—her child who was only months older than my own. Rightfully outraged, she took the day off work to make calls to her landlord, demanding they fix it. The landlord refused. She continued to fight, taking another day away from her job to make calls and go to offices around town. Her employer fired her for missing too many days of work. The landlord continued to refuse to fix the dilapidated ceiling, and my neighbor was ultimately evicted.

Not long after this, I began to notice news headlines with story after story of Black men and boys being killed by white police officers: Michael Brown, Tamir Rice, Eric Garner, and in my own city, Milwaukee, Dontre Hamilton was murdered because the police felt fourteen shots was an acceptable way to soothe the discomfort of a Starbucks employee uncomfortable with Hamilton's presence in an adjacent park.

A year or so after that, I picked up a bookmark at church one Sunday morning challenging people to read and pray through Bible verses on immigration for forty days. I'd never really thought about immigration before, so I followed the reading plan. I became aware of how incredibly difficult it is for people from certain countries to immigrate to the United States, and that for so many the legal pathways simply do not exist, or the wait is so long that it is nonsensical. I learned that most of our food is harvested by undocumented migrant farmers,[1] and since they're often paid under the table, they are also often wildly underpaid and mistreated.[2]

"Liberty and justice for all" gradually began to feel like an aspiration at best, if not an outright myth, a selective liberation for some to pacify a people swimming in waters of exploitation and injustice.

In this chapter, we're going to look at the story we've been formed by regarding race, which is really a question about what it means to bear the image of God, and to whom exactly that status applies.

THE STORY THAT FORMS US: WHO COUNTS AS HUMAN?

One of the first questions that arose in the formation of a new nation was the question of whose voice would count in the decision-making process. Before the American Revolution, Indigenous people, colonizers, refugees, enslaved persons, and indentured servants lived together tenuously, if not violently, but these categories were not set in stone.[3] The binding and immovable classifications we impose on one another today through the construct of race had not yet been invented. But as European colonizers and religious refugees began to impose their ideas about order and governance throughout the land, they established rules that allowed certain persons a seat at the decision-making table and denied a seat to others.

These rules were not constructed in isolation, nor did they appeal primarily to political ideology for their basis. The so-called Age of Discovery was ushered in by a theological mandate from the Roman Catholic Church in the form of papal bulls.[4] This series of documents called for the "restraint," "domination" and "vanquishment" of the "infidels," meaning people in Africa and the "New World" who did not follow the Christian faith.[5] These documents laid the framework for the Doctrine of Discovery, a theological mandate that justified European colonizers to seize lands and convert or kill whomever they found in their path.

Despite the warring between Catholic and Protestant churches, Protestant laypeople and pastors alike adopted the Doctrine of Discovery as a means of sanctifying their actions in the New World. In his 1855 text *Our Country: Its Possible Future and Its Present Crisis*, Protestant clergyman Josiah Strong wrote, "There can be no reasonable doubt that North America is to be the home of the Anglo-Saxon, the principle seat of his power, the center of his life and influence. . . . The world enter[s] upon a new stage of its history—*the final competition of races for which the Anglo-Saxon is being schooled.*" The destiny of Anglo-Saxons was, Strong argued, a matter of "survival of the fittest." Strong wrote, "Nothing can save the inferior race but a ready and pliant assimilation," even as he admitted that their "extinction . . . appears probable."[6] In other words, as writer Kelly Brown Douglas notes, the contention and presumption was that "the Anglo-Saxon race will be the last race standing."[7]

Most Christians were unconcerned with such a stark pursuit of power by some at the expense of others because they assumed God had structured society like a pyramid and that contentment with one's created place in that pyramid was virtuous and good.[8] Social stratification, even to the degree that the humanity of some people was denied, was merely a representation of what people believed to be true on a cosmic scale. Famed puritan preacher Cotton Mather wrote to enslaved Africans that they were "better fed & better clothed & better managed by far, than you would be, if you were your own men," insisting that the enslaved men and women could obtain their salvation and have their "souls washed white" by obeying their enslavers.[9]

The writers and signers of the U.S. Constitution drafted a vision of the world in which Europeans, and in particular European men, formed the top of the hierarchy, granting them rights to own land (and other humans), to vote, and to run for public office. By eliminating the rights of European women, relegating all people of African descent to three-fifths humanity, and completely denying the humanity of Indigenous people, the Constitution *theologically* functions to bolster the belief that European men are more godlike than anyone else.

While there were some who opposed the stratification of society on the basis of race, most Christians did not fight against the rising power of European colonizers over and against all other people groups inhabiting the continent. In some instances, laws enacted in Europe to uphold Christian values of mutuality and to prioritize the mystical body of Christ were subverted with new laws in the colonies to create space for the construct of racial hierarchy.

For example, English common law forbade Christians from enslaving other Christians, but this law was not readily enforced in the colonies. In 1667, colonial Virginia decreed that "the conferring of baptism doth not alter the condition of the person as to his bondage." This made it legal for Virginians not only to enslave people being trafficked from Africa, but to pursue enslavement as a missionary venture, since conversion of enslaved people posed no threat to the wealth of slaveholders.[10]

English common law also dictated that children's legal status followed that of their father. But after a biracial Christian woman, Elizabeth Key, sued Virginia for her and her child's freedom, Virginia legislated that children's legal status would follow that of their mother. This law further deprived enslaved African women of their humanity and created economic incentive for the European men who owned them to rape them without consequence.[11]

This political and theological framework of white, land-owning, male dominance carried the United States through a century of systemic enslavement of millions of people of African descent. Many white congregations who were pro-abolition during and after the Civil War were rendered ill-equipped to do the reframing and repentance necessary for conciliation with African Americans because they neglected to address the theological aspects of this framework along with its political aspects. The slave apologists of the era dug in to defend their direct, literal readings of Scripture, and to support the theology of a divinely inspired hierarchy.

After Reconstruction abruptly ended, slavery apologists shifted their tone slightly, but continued to promote a literal interpretation of Scripture—an approach to reading the text that condoned enslavement. These leaders planted churches, started colleges, and funded printing houses and magazines. The institutions they launched ascribed to a philosophy of "Head, heart, and hand," an approach designed to teach the whole person. But while the underlying philosophy is beautiful and necessary, "Head, heart, and hand" had another agenda. The philosophy was steeped in racialized bias and white supremacy, and envisioned Christian education and vocational training as a way to uphold poor whites in the South, "that last stronghold . . . of 'pure Anglo-Saxon blood.'"[12]

After World War II, African American veterans pressed in to their "Double V" hopes for victory abroad against the Axis powers and victory at home against Jim Crow. They sought to make good on the benefits promised them during the war.

Victory had been won against the fascist regimes abroad, and now the veterans mobilized for victory against racism at home.[13] White pastors and church leaders, for their part, ignored the Double V campaign, despite the support it garnered from African American church leaders,[14] a stance that deepened the gulf between the Black and white church in the United States.

Martin Luther King Jr.'s leadership in the civil rights movement proved to be a conundrum for evangelicals. King's Scripture-soaked rhetoric would seemingly fall in line with even the staunchest white evangelical adherence to Scripture, yet white clergy were largely dismissive of King's work, citing the concern that addressing racism on a systemic level would promote communism.[15] In response to King's march on Selma, Virginia pastor Jerry Falwell unleashed the most significant sermon of his career. "Preachers are not called to be politicians but soul winners," he declared in a 1964 sermon entitled "Ministers and Marches." His rhetoric played easily to the revivalism of the moment, and echoed the popular idea of the pure, spiritual Christianity that featured a personal Jesus who would come live a quiet, private life in the hearts of true believers.

Billy Graham, playing off increasing white anxieties about the civil rights movement of the 1950s and '60s, proclaimed that true believers would be snatched out of the turmoil on earth when Christ returned, an event that Graham insisted would occur soon. Everything from the development of hydrogen bombs to the spread of communism to the rise of feminism and civil rights was seen as a sign of the impending judgment day.[16]

White Christians struggled to imagine a world in which Black people were recognized as beautiful, intelligent, and free and equal in the sight of the law; and in which women of all races were competent, thoughtful, and equal to men. Instead they clung fearfully to the idea that the world must be coming to an end. In reality, these white evangelicals were facing down the dead end of their own stunted imaginations.

In 1970, the federal government began to crack down on enforcing the anti-segregation legislation of the 1960s. Any educational institution with a policy of denying admittance on the basis of race risked the loss of its tax-exempt status. This caused quite a controversy, and at the center of it was Bob Jones University, a Christian college in Greenville, South Carolina.[17] BJU fought for the ability to keep its tax-exempt status and its segregationist values, but the court said no. In response, Bob Jones and several other prominent leaders of Christian schools and churches—notably Jerry Falwell of Liberty University—gathered to form a political strategy for fighting for the racial "integrity" of their institutions. They called this new movement the Moral Majority.

This coalition of pro-segregationist Christians, united under the more palatable banners of "pro-life, pro-family" values, organized one of the most powerful and committed voting blocs in the United States. The election of Ronald Reagan marked an enormous victory for the Moral Majority, but Reagan's election, and his commitment to building on President Nixon's War on Drugs, had devastating consequences for communities of color.[18] Once again, white Christians had united around accumulating more for themselves—more power, more resources—to the detriment of their Black and brown siblings in Christ.

THE BIBLE SAYS . . .

It can be precarious to read the biblical text as a guide to race. The Bible does not directly speak about race, because race—as we think of it today—did not exist in the ancient Near East context of the biblical authors. While the colonialists certainly employed Scripture in support of their racialized tactics, the idea of race was developed by them as justification for seeking to subjugate people indigenous to North America and those trafficked from Africa. What we can extrapolate from the Bible about race comes from texts which speak to social class and ethnicity—both of which are closely tied to the construct of race.

The authors of the Bible were largely, though not exclusively, living at the margins of their societies, not in positions of power, and they wrote for people who also were largely on the margins. In much of the biblical narrative, Israel is enslaved, at war, or exiled. The vast majority of the biblical narrative occurs while the people of God were subjected to the Egyptian, Persian, Babylonian, and Roman Empires. So when a biblical text speaks of welcoming outsiders, or caring for someone outside one's own ethnic group, the authors are not calling for benevolence on the part of a wealthy benefactor toward an impoverished person. They are advocating for taking the risk of loving and caring for someone who has exploited them and their people. For modern readers approaching the Bible from social positions valued and empowered by society at large— white, male, educated, currently able-bodied, wealthy or middle class—we have internal work to do as readers before we will be able to read the text with integrity.

There are examples throughout Scripture in which people cross bounds of ethnicity or social class for the purposes of God or to receive the blessing of God. Rahab, a Canaanite who lived in Jericho, hid Israelite spies scouting the Promised Land; she and her family were spared in the destruction of Jericho (Joshua 2). Ruth, a Moabite woman, returned to Israel with Naomi, her Israelite mother-in-law, and she found favor with Boaz, whom she ended up marrying.[19] In the damning narrative of David's rape of Bathsheba, we're told that Bathsheba's husband was a Hittite, a detail which suggests that Bathsheba may have been a Hittite as well (2 Samuel 11).[20] Bathsheba later became the mother of King Solomon and sat at his right hand as a source of council. (1 Kings 2:19).[21]

In the Gospels, Jesus healed the Syrophoenician woman's daughter and proclaimed the woman's faith to be greater than any in Israel (Mark 7:24-30; Matthew 15:21-28). The Roman centurion who sought Jesus out to heal his servant received a similar commendation of faith (Matthew 8:5-13). In Samaria, Jesus spoke with a woman at the well, and entrusted her with the news that he is the Messiah (John 4:1-42).

The remainder of the Christian Scriptures are punctuated with stories of unexpected relationships between people of different ethnic groups and social classes. Philip baptizes a eunuch from Ethiopia (Acts 8:26-40). Peter eats with Cornelius, a Gentile, and bears witness as the Holy Spirit falls on the whole household (Acts 10:1-48). Paul audaciously writes to the Galatian church that it no longer matters if you're Jewish or Greek, all are welcomed into the people of God (Galatians 3:28). In his letter to Philemon, Paul urges the master of the house to welcome back the runaway enslaved Onesimus, not as a slave, but as a brother (Philemon 16).

There is abundant evidence across the canon that the movement of those seeking after God is toward those who are considered outsiders and who have been devalued by society. These instances, while not directly speaking about the construct of race, can guide our ethics and engagement around race in the church today.

UNLEARNING AND RETURNING: PERSONAL
Decolonizing our faith

We all come to the conversation of unlearning the stereotypes and social norms placed on us by the construct of race from different places. The work I must do as a white woman is different from that of my Latinx, Asian American, Pacific Islander, Black and African American, and Indigenous friends and siblings in Christ. So as we turn our attention toward conformity to Christ—seeking connection over consumption—with regard to race, I am going to introduce you to some folks whose work, friendship, and journey have influenced my own. I encourage you to read through each of these accounts—even if the person writing does not share your social location. We all benefit when we learn to listen to one another well.

First, I want to introduce you to my friend Irene, who has taught me so much about how both my family and my history form me, but also about how to speak up bravely and subvert the expectations of my formative community.

No one can tell my story
Irene Cho

My mother has been lecturing me my entire life that I should never fool myself into believing I am anything other than Asian, and in particular Korean. No matter how much I wish to assimilate and escape, she told me, there is no escaping my facial features, skin tone, and even hair color (believe me, Asians have to deal with a whole set of items when it comes to trying to make ourselves blond). I would cringe whenever she said these words because they stung. I wanted to be white.

And why not? Everyone in my world was white. The books I read, the movies and television shows I watched, the music I listened to, and the preachers I followed. I was well into my thirties before I began to accept my mother's words encouraging me to embrace who God created me to be, to not apologize for it, and most importantly, to be proud. But this journey was a slow progression. After all, the respected voices, leaders, and prophets whom I was taught were the pinnacle of wisdom are all white men. Until recently this was acceptable to me because my entire subconscious and conscious belief system was formed by the idea of the white church as the guiding light leading the charge toward holiness.

Yet as I've expanded my education and knowledge, reading new content, listening to more preachers, and finding a community of friends and colleagues with whom I can journey, I've realized just how ingrained whiteness has been in my faith. The opportunity to lead an urban leadership training program allowed me to sit at the feet of some of the most brilliant professors of color who have challenged my assumption that "white makes it right." I have had wonderful opportunities to develop my mind in a more critically thoughtful way and have learned not to blindly accept what I am told about the standard or what is "normal." Every day is an exercise of deconstructing the world and my default perspective by asking questions: Who is being featured in this commercial or television show and why? Who is speaking? Who were the people in charge of making this decision? How many people of color are also gathering in this space I am about to enter? What are the perspective and assumptions of the storyteller? Who is fiscally benefiting from this item being sold? Who were the people who made these items I am purchasing?

This deconstruction is sometimes exhausting work. But it's necessary. To flatten our faith to a singular voice and story is insulting to the complex tapestry of God's creation. God is not a white man. God is beyond. And She has created the world and all the beings in it to each have a story to tell that will enhance each other. I now know no one can tell my story, and most importantly, I know that my story is valuable and important because I am God's creation.

Next, meet Michelle Higgins. I first encountered Michelle's work when she gave one of the best sermons I have ever heard at InterVarsity's Urbana Student Missions Conference in 2015. Michelle's keen vision for equity in the kingdom of God continues to challenge and sharpen me, particularly with regard to holding the spiritual conviction of justice together with the embodied witness of organizing for it.

I know where true power lives
Michelle Higgins

Beloved Community, as Dr. Martin Luther King Jr. envisioned it, is an achievable harmony, one that indicts addiction to wealth and power by pleading the case of humility and truth. While pursuing commitments to gender and racial justice in evangelical spaces, I have never heard so many people use the words of Jesus, "The poor will be with us always," as an excuse to hoard wealth and ignore people who have been oppressed. This oppression is perpetrated by an enemy of our own making, an enemy that we can defeat in our day. Through observing communal corruption and injustice, I have learned to cling to the practice of personal and communal confession. Colonized theology focuses on a daily life that exhibits a "personal" walk with Jesus—private prayer-closet piety that exists for the sake of holiness in one's own household. There is no doubt about the importance of these practices; even the great James Cone pressed upon his students and readers that true liberation begins in the home. This quietism, however, is revealed in Scripture as incomplete for living into Christlikeness.

As Jesus intentionally sought desolate places to pray, to escape the attention generated by his own fame, and to experience union as God with the Spirit and with the Creator, he showed the purpose of preparation in this practice—Jesus prayed and privately contemplated because he led a public life.

Jesus is the reason that I engage in civic life and work for justice in solidarity with oppressed people. He is the reason that I can simultaneously demand political influence for marginalized people yet place no amount of ultimate confidence in political power. Because I know where true power lives, I can demand that the authorities in my day—in my city and my country—wield their power for the defeat of racism, militarism, poverty, and arrogance.

Jesus teaches us that there are many evils that can be cast out only through fasting and prayer. I am learning that the decolonized versions of "fasting and prayer" are the spiritual practices of confessional truth, grace, hope, accountability, and humility. These practices embolden me to faithful action toward God's definition of justice: a community of wholly beloved created beings who do not lack for opportunities to thrive, and who share in loving celebration, mutual sacrifice, and protection from exploitation. Such a community provides access to authority figures who live and govern as equals with their constituents, and the right to challenge any human powers that dehumanize before they empathize.

None of these practices imply perfection, and all of them emphasize the elements of a community that are possible right now, in our day. My faith demands that my life display my commitments: I teach protest as spiritual practice, I long to fix my failures, I mourn the losses that occur at my own hands, and I demand justice when my community suffers loss at the hands of the authorities. I preach dignity for the poor and honor for the invisible. I do not hide the failures of my family from my children, and I hold space for celebrating the glories of God that have brought every victory in my history—and every victory to come.

I met Karen during an Enneagram workshop in 2017 (a love for discussing the Enneagram, a personality typology model, is one of the fastest ways to ensure lasting friendship with me). As we got to know each other better, I learned that Karen worked with mobilizing churches to help with refugee resettlement and immigration reform. I deeply valued her perspective on what was happening in the political moment at the time. Dehumanizing rhetoric was being lobbed at asylum seekers and migrants on the southern U.S. border, and Karen was calling us to see Christ not primarily in the white Christians trying to help, but in the Latinx people who were being detained.

Brown, like us

Karen González

"Jesus was not white," my New Testament professor said emphatically. On the screen beside him appeared a picture of a dark-skinned man with a beard. He reminded me of any one of a dozen of my adult male relatives. I had honestly never thought about the fact that Jesus, as a Jewish man from the Middle East, had brown skin and dark hair.

When I pictured Jesus in my head, he always looked like the statue on the cross in my childhood Catholic parish in Guatemala. He had white skin, blue eyes, and European features. In fact, all the saints in the parish were white. Even without any instruction, I internalized the lie that white people are superior, so of course our God had to be white and couldn't possibly be brown like us.

Throughout my journey of faith, I've had to unlearn not only the idea that Jesus was white but also the lie that the culture and faith expression of white people is the ideal we should strive for. Even though all my required seminary classes taught me the theology of white men, I had to learn that the Spirit of God permeates all cultures and reveals God's truth through the dark-skinned grandmother who passed down her faith to me, although she had little education.

Day by day I continue to unlearn, not just through the reshaping of my imagination but through asking questions of the Bible that I was never taught to ask: For whom is the gospel good news? How does this passage speak to people's liberation? What does this passage say about power? What are the parallels in my society? Who is in power, and who is marginalized?

I know that who Jesus is and what he did transcends his skin color and unique facial features. But I cannot deny how deeply meaningful and transformative it was to learn that he was a dark-skinned person. I often reflect on the God who became flesh and took on brown flesh even though he could have been any color he wanted; reflecting on it reinforces the truth that brown-skinned people are image-bearers of God and rewrites the narrative for us. We matter to God, even if not to our society. And God has endowed us with dignity and worth and invites us to be part of the family as we are.

Repenting from the idolatry of whiteness

I come from a long line of women who led the church, although I didn't realize this for a long time. I grew up walking past a faded photograph of my great-grandmother among the small crew of founding members of the United Methodist church I was born into. As Sunday school superintendent, my grandmother would poke her head into my Sunday school room and note attendance over five hundred times during my childhood. I grew up watching boxes of stickers and decorations, craft supplies, and balloons arrive from mail-order catalogs while my mother was coordinating vacation Bible school. When I felt the Holy Spirit tug my heart toward ministry in college, I should not have been shocked. I stand on the shoulders of the women who went before me.

The shoulders I stand on are not without fault, though. The United Methodist church that my great-grandmother helped to found built a fellowship hall the same year I was born— 1987. A major funding source for the project was the local Ku Klux Klan chapter. I may come from a line of women who built the church, but there are some elements of what they built that need to be torn down, and that work of deconstructing and critiquing begins with me and inside me. Engaging in anti-racist work means I am committed to combating the racism within myself, as well as in the systems and structures of this world.[22]

I stumbled into conversations about racial justice in college while working at a nonprofit. I was one of the few white people on the after-school program staff. It was 2009, and Barack Obama was about to be inaugurated as the forty-fourth president of the United States. I hadn't voted for Obama, but his policies and rhetoric intrigued me. The program director decided that on Inauguration Day we would all gather in the auditorium and watch a replay of the ceremony—everyone from the first-grade class through the high school students. I was disgruntled. What kind of kid was going to sit and watch a presidential inauguration?

The day arrived and the kids filed into the auditorium. Some were dressed up in church clothes, which seemed odd to me. My boss, the program director, was wearing a T-shirt with Barack Obama's name and face printed on it, along with his new title: 44th President of the United States. I was suddenly aware that there was something big happening, and I was missing it. As we played a recording of the inauguration, the students sat in rapt silence and then broke into deafening cheers when the swearing in ended. My boss and coworkers cried. I tried to stay focused on the ceremony, and not on my shock at the apparent magnitude of the moment for the others in the room. As we left the auditorium, the hallways filled with kids' voices singing, "My president is Black!" I was stunned, and curious. I never cared much about who was president as a child. I decided to listen closely to my coworkers and the students to try to figure out why this inauguration was such a big deal.

My resolve to continue to listen closely would be tested in the years after that emotional day in 2009. In 2010 I moved from the rural community where I'd grown up, and my job at the nonprofit, to a disinvested neighborhood in Milwaukee where I was in the minority racially and socioeconomically. During the rise of the movement for Black lives, white friends and family members back in my hometown responded to my social media posts by saying, "Not all cops are bad." I knew from experience that getting pulled over in my new neighborhood would involve at least two officers, one on either side of the car, and a glaring flashlight in my face if it was dark. In my case, the blinding light was followed by a shift in demeanor, an apology, and the second officer returning to their car. I'd been pulled over more times in the couple of years I'd lived on Forty-Fifth Street than I had in all the rest of my driving career. Mostly, the officers were concerned that I would make it home safely, even though I was on my own block. Our president was Black, and we had all been raised to not "see color," but I couldn't deny the reality that the paleness of my skin prompted a different reaction from those sworn to serve and protect my new neighborhood.

These experiences and the generous, costly work of my friends of color have steadied and sharpened my commitment to unlearning and recovering from whiteness—a social construct used to hoard power for people of European descent and to elevate our norms as ideal for all people. I have had to become aware of how I resist or cooperate with systems and ideologies of white supremacy. When I embrace and propagate stereotypes of my neighbors of color, I am cooperating with white supremacy. When I expect to be thanked or congratulated or thought of as a "good person" for reading books by authors of color or for showing up to events led by people of color, I am cooperating with white supremacy. When I avoid certain parts of town because they feel dangerous or choose to disengage from a hard conversation about race with another white person because it's uncomfortable, I am cooperating with white supremacy.

Once I become aware of how I am cooperating with whiteness, I actively begin to work against it. Will I choose to be humble and to listen to others, knowing that there is so much I do not know because the privilege afforded me has insulated me from reality? Will I choose to see God not as a white man on a throne, but as the fierce and dedicated Latina mother who crosses all borders in hopes of her children flourishing? Will I learn to see Jesus as a man with brown skin and a brow weathered from growing up under the oppression of an empire, instead of a Jesus with blond hair and soft blue eyes who lives in the White House? These are questions I must engage with daily to continue to decolonize my faith and move toward solidarity with my neighbor.

I've come to understand that whiteness is an idolatrous force. White people, for the most part, would not directly say they're more godlike than other races, but functionally we act in this way. Whiteness convinces people that the world should orient around fulfilling their individual desires and eliminating their personal pain or discomfort. As a white person, I expect that my complaints will be taken seriously and resolved quickly. I expect that my opinions will be validated and understood by everyone else. I expect that any store I walk into will sell the personal care products I use, the right makeup foundation for my skin tone, and the snacks I like to eat. While shopping, I expect to do so in peace, without being flagged by security guards or other store employees.

While whiteness is a system bigger than just me, and because therefore I will likely benefit from my pale skin for the duration of my life, I can actively resist the temptation to exploit this privilege every day. When I notice a group taking my words more seriously than others, I choose to make an effort to solicit the input of any people of color present and back them up. I make choices to learn from leaders of color, to read authors of color, to enroll my child in ballet classes through a Black-owned dance studio. The bias I grew up with tells me all kinds of lies about people of color, but slowly, day by day, I am choosing to learn to see the world anew.

UNLEARNING AND RETURNING: PEOPLE
Repairing the breach of church complicity

The history of the church in the United States with respect to race is damning. Protestant clergy and Great Awakening preachers were instrumental in upholding and enshrining racial hierarchies in the United States. Christians today cannot turn a blind eye to the errors of our past and move forward as if nothing happened. So-called "colorblindness" helps no one. We cannot follow Christ in choosing connection over consumption so long as our arms are full of prejudices that warp the truth, power we have hoarded, and wealth we have stolen.

In his book *The Color of Compromise*, historian Jemar Tisby recounts the church's complicity with racism in the United States. Notably, every major denomination split over the issue of slavery during the Civil War era. During Reconstruction and the Jim Crow era, lynchings were often planned for Sunday afternoons and held near or on the premises of a church (sometimes, most cruelly, at Black churches) so that larger crowds could gather.[23] During the early 1900s, when specific theological resources were being distributed for free to white pastors and seminaries, Black pastors and training institutions were excluded, effectively codifying evangelicalism as a white movement.[24]

While there have been some moves on a denominational level to state apologies for or to issue resolutions against such evils, there are far too many people filling the pews on Sunday mornings who have no knowledge of this history, nor of how (or if) their denomination has done anything to correct this legacy. I once attended a talk by Navajo activist and author Mark Charles about a book he coauthored, *Unsettling Truths*. As he reminded us, where there is no common story, there can be no forward movement together.[25] The church is at a standstill on race because white Christians still struggle to tell the truth about our complicity.

During the 1990s and early 2000s there was an assumption that race relations were generally getting better among many white churches—evangelical or otherwise. Movements for multiethnic/multiracial/multicultural congregations sprang up, and talk of racial reconciliation moved from justice-centered circles on the fringe of Christian networks to the mainstream. But this does not mean all is well, or that the only thing left to do to overcome racism in our ranks is to diversify our congregations.

The challenge of racism in the post–civil rights era is that the laws on the books lie about our progress. Legally, there is no discrimination based on race. Legally, public schools are integrated. Legally, neighborhoods are not designed for racial homogeneity. Practically, though, the day-to-day reality of people of color is another story.

As articulated in the history and tradition portion of this chapter, the errors of the church in relationship to race have been largely systemic, and as such must be addressed not only on a personal level but on a corporate level as well. This is not just for the sake of social justice, or to cultivate a diverse image. This is essential work to engage in order to faithfully follow Jesus and participate in the kingdom of God here on earth as it is in heaven. In the Christian Scriptures, a diverse gathering of people working to navigate mutuality and equity within their midst is interpreted as evidence of the Holy Spirit at work. That portrayal of a Spirit-filled Christian community is a far cry from the salvation tally-keeping and gathering of audiences to fill large auditoriums that many evangelicals tout as success symbols today.

Theologian and scholar Christena Cleveland notes that while we can initially meet God in a homogenous space, we cannot follow Jesus in a homogenous community, because God is—in essence—diversity.[26] Yet for over fifty years in the United States, a primary church growth strategy has taught congregations to target homogenous groups and capitalize on the affinity of people with similar life experiences and social locations. This not only malforms our communities, but also makes us forgetful of the complexity and mystery of the triune God. Movements for "diverse" congregations or church leadership have become increasingly popular in recent years, but often without congregations and denominations fully taking into account the harm that homogeneity has wrought in the church over the years, and the potential for ongoing harm if assimilation is required instead of fostering true diversity.

Approaches to diversity within groups of people must be built on a foundation of mutual respect and fearless truth-telling—which means that people who have dictated the terms of the conversation over the years (usually white people) will need to take a seat and learn to follow. Conversations must be nuanced and must bear in mind that there is a cost to diversity for everyone involved. For those whom society has afforded privilege, the cost of decentering their experience and preferences will likely feel uncomfortable and perhaps evoke responses of anger. As Jesus notes, it's worthwhile to count the cost before embarking on this work (Luke 14:25-33), lest well-intentioned but ill-prepared white people perpetuate harm.

For the majority group in a congregation or community, it is helpful to become aware of their own values, biases, and assumptions about the "right" way to gather or "do church." These practices are often coded not only within denominations, but also along racial, socioeconomic, geographic, and educational lines. When a community is unaware that they have a way of doing things that reflects their own cultural preferences, they are in danger of dismissing a neutral, but different, way of doing things as wrong, unbiblical, or bad.

For some communities, even this exercise of acknowledging and mapping their values and biases may reveal the best place to start in moving toward a more equitable and diverse community. A congregation may find it helpful to look up their denomination's official stance on racism or white supremacy, and then begin to work through the implications of that statement for their own community. If a congregation exists outside of a denominational structure, accounting for the history and the policies about race within the congregation is a good place to start.

UNLEARNING AND RETURNING: PUBLIC
Public sin requires public correction

It is fundamentally necessary that our work for racial justice not remain in the personal or church arenas alone. Race served as the basis for Native American extradition and genocide, which is the reason why the United States possesses the geographic area it does today. This is an act of public sin, so it must be addressed on a public level. From the foundations of our nation, race served as the basis for chattel slavery and thus the basis for the U.S. economy. This is an act of public sin, so it must be addressed on a public level. Race served as the defining measure for Japanese American internment during World War II and for setting immigration ratios on the law books. As I write this, it is the determining factor for which people will be detained by Immigration and Customs Enforcement—regardless of citizenship or legal status![27] Race determines who is separated from their children and who is placed in detention centers for exercising their human right to seek asylum. Every aspect of our public life has been touched by the ideology of race, so unlearning the construct of race and responding to Christ's invitation to become Beloved Community *requires* public witness.

Truth-telling

As theologian Stanley Hauerwas might put it, "The first job of a Christian is to tell the truth." Public witness means pressing for and working toward truth-telling on a massive scale.

Activist, author, and 2020 presidential candidate Mark Charles is leading a grassroots movement to press for a nationwide "truth and conciliation" council in 2021.[28] You can engage in public truth-telling on a local level as well, though. If you are a parent or guardian, ask the teachers and administrators in your child's school about how the history of colonization is taught, including whether Columbus Day is observed or whether they honor Indigenous Peoples' Day, and how the narrative around Thanksgiving is presented. Ask about the ways the school observes Black History Month (February); Asian Pacific American Heritage Month (May), Hispanic Heritage Month (September 15–October 15), and Native American Heritage Month (November).

Contact your city or state government to press for the observance of Indigenous Peoples' Day in place of Columbus Day. Take the time to learn about any statues or monuments in your community, the people they memorialize, and how. Consider organizing in your community to take action as needed to more faithfully represent history in your public spaces.

Reparations

In the spring of 2019, the U.S. House of Representatives held a hearing on reparations, inviting author Ta-Nehisi Coates to testify.[29] Reparations, the making of amends for a wrongdoing by paying money to those who have been wronged, can feel like a challenging conversation at times, but it's a necessary undertaking for our public witness. The vision of justice provided by Scripture is always restorative and transformative.

In a country where our economy was founded on a trafficked and enslaved labor force, for there to be anything close to the biblical idea of justice enacted means reparations are a must. (I'll say more about reparations in a later chapter.)

Justice system reforms

It is well documented that the criminal justice system in the United States disproportionately affects communities of color, and Black communities in particular.[30] Paying attention to proposed legislation in your local community or your state about issues like cash bail, mandatory sentencing, and "banning the box" for those seeking employment after a felony conviction is one way to allow our faith to inform our public engagement with the justice system.

6

FORGIVE US OUR DEBTS
Connection over Consumption in Finances

The number one thing couples fight over is money," warned our premarital counselor. He spit out the word *money* as if it were bitter and handed us a sleek binder full of CDs and a book that matched. "These will teach you to manage your money *God's* way." A couple of weeks later, on a road trip from our then-home in West Virginia to Wisconsin, we listened to the entire series of CDs.

I hated it.

The bright man with a southern drawl talked about how reckless debt was and how people who spent years paying off debts were paying a "stupid tax." He advocated for using only cash for large purchases. "Cash is king!" he insisted. "Isn't Jesus supposed to be king?" I smirked at my fiancé.

To be fair, it wasn't *all* bad advice. One lesson gave instructions for making a budget and another talked about the importance of speaking openly with your spouse about finances, especially before making large purchases. The speaker talked about the price point—a few hundred dollars—at which he committed to talking with his wife before buying something. My fiancé and I looked at each other wide-eyed. "Anything over twenty bucks?" he suggested. Given how significant twenty dollars was in our bank accounts at the time, I agreed.

We muddled our way through our first few years of marriage. Some months we sat down faithfully, as instructed by the man on the CD, for a "budget meeting." Unlike the man on the CD, I insisted this meeting happen at a coffee shop where I could order a latte and cookies to ease the pain of being forced to look at our finances.

We worked hard to live within our means, and we both had the privilege of graduating from college without a significant amount of student loan debt. My job at our church, while not salaried at the time, did provide our housing. Our family members and many friends also had enough economic privilege to offer us their used furniture when they were updating, which we gratefully accepted.

I had no reason to hate talking about money as much as I did. I had been afforded every privilege growing up—parents who taught me how to track a bank account (and who helped bail me out when I incurred overdraft fees in high school), college scholarships that covered a large chunk of my tuition, and rent-free housing in young adulthood. Even with all that, scarcity plagued my thoughts. It seemed there would never be enough. Our furniture remained mismatched, and not always the style I would have liked, unlike our friends whose living rooms were well coordinated and Pinterest-worthy. Our cars were ten-plus years old and required regular repairs.

"Debt is dumb," the man's voice from the CD echoed in my mind. I agreed with that statement. Friends were often stressed about how long they were going to be paying off their loans. Others were working in jobs they hated to make minimum payments on loans they'd acquired in order to learn skills they were now unable to use in the workplace. I didn't think that anyone was saying debt was a *smart* idea, but perhaps it wasn't as easy to avoid as the man on the CD seemed to think.

It didn't seem to me that avoiding debt was always a choice. In my neighborhood, we had to drive three miles to get to the nearest bank, but we could walk down the street to cash our check for a fee at the payday loan store. For my neighbors, many of whom did not own cars, the three-mile trek to the bank via bus was tough to fit in; their few hours off, which they spent trying to rest after their second- or third-shift jobs, were usually during conventional business hours.

Other friends had been advised by their college financial aid offices to take out loans—"You'll get a job and pay them back before you know it!" But we graduated from college in 2006, so when the recession of 2008 hit, we were the first ones fired—if we'd even managed to find jobs at that point. Meanwhile, the interest rates on our student loans climbed ever higher.

I grew up thinking that faithfulness to Christ in my finances was as simple as consistently giving 10 percent of my allowance, and later my paycheck, to the church. My inner idealist wanted to take a pass on hard conversations about money and to trust that God would provide somehow. Cattle on a thousand hills and all that jazz. I've become increasingly convinced, though, that there are some very important conversations we need to have about money—both as individuals and institutionally. Scripture and church history are full of examples of simplicity and generous redistribution of resources, of people grappling with how to steward wealth faithfully, and of people striving to overturn systems that perpetuate poverty. Yet when we look at the bulk of conversations around money in the church in the United States, most of them center on charitable giving, and perhaps on the importance of a household budget. How did the story of faithfulness with our finances shift from a vision of no one in our midst being in need to a practice of looking out for our own security? Let's look back.

THE STORY THAT FORMS US

Early in the formation of the United States, itinerant preachers such as John Winthrop captivated the spiritual imagination of the colonizers, relocating the authority to interpret biblical texts from local communities to individual traveling orators.[1] These traveling orators inspired local pastors and stoked the fears of congregations, urging them to greater degrees of holiness. While authority was less formally structured and certainly less centralized than in the Catholic and Anglican churches of Europe, systems and structures of authority were still alive and well in the land of "holy experiments."

Building a godly society meant upholding a proper hierarchy, and "success lay in deference and harmony."[2] While the so-called New World was seen as a land of opportunity, there was also a moral imperative not to challenge hierarchies of rich and poor, enslaved and free, because this stratification was understood to be the will of God.

Throughout the better part of the first hundred and fifty years of U.S. history, these God-ordained "proper hierarchies" were discerned using methods of theology that were akin to the scientific method. Scripture was seen as the plain word of God, and the "self-evident" propositions of the text were believed to be "clear."[3] The thing about a plain, self-evident reading of the text, though, is that any piece of Scripture can easily be ripped from the greater context and manipulated to support whatever ends the reader is seeking to advance.

A plain reading of the text was used by the Virginia Company to bolster their business charter, all the while enslaving people trafficked from Africa and forcing Indigenous people off the land where they lived.[4] A plain reading of Scripture was used to support the country's westward expansion and the continued displacement of Indigenous people. It was used to bolster pro-enslavement arguments during the Reconstruction era, and used to discredit the voices of women organizing for suffrage in the early 1900s.[5] In 1919, this method of appealing to the plain, literal meaning of Scripture was codified in a series of theological essays called *The Fundamentals: A Testimony to the Truth*, which was distributed to virtually every white Protestant pastor in America.[6]

During the slow, arduous recovery from the Great Depression, white evangelical leaders who had coalesced around *The Fundamentals* and the "plain" reading of the text they supported attracted an increasing number of people into their movement. The certainty with which these men read the Bible and their no-nonsense leadership calmed fears.[7] When President Franklin Roosevelt took office in 1933, implementing his New Deal policies, resistance from leaders and communities shaped by *The Fundamentals* was swift and severe. Their opposition was laced with worry that the New Deal was "overbearing" and "bureaucratic" and that it threatened to squash what they saw as clear biblical mandates to hard work and proper hierarchy.[8] Popular evangelist Billy Sunday warned against the New Deal policies, likening them to the "serpentine coils of this communistic, socialistic, atheistic, [*sic*] monster."[9]

But Roosevelt was a practicing Episcopalian, and his New Deal was informed by his faith every bit as much as his opponents were driven by theirs.[10] Roosevelt embraced Christian rhetoric, framing campaign speeches as "preaching a sermon" rather than "talking politics."[11] When it came time to deliver his first inaugural address, he included so many references to Scripture that the National Bible Press followed up by publishing a chart linking his speech to the verses he referenced from the Bible.[12] Such use of the Bible and of Christian tradition did not earn Roosevelt many fans among evangelicals, though, and he quickly became "a stand-in for all the progressive attitudes that seemed to be turning Americans away from more traditional family-based values."[13]

Amid this religious, political, and financial quagmire, an itinerant preacher, Billy Graham, began to make his ascent into the public eye. Graham was influenced by *The Fundamentals*, with its plain reading of Scripture and enshrinement of social hierarchy. The poor, Graham insisted, did not need government assistance; rather, "their greatest need is Christ. Give them the Gospel of love and grace first and they will clean themselves up, educate themselves, and better their economic conditions."[14]

Graham's influence would stretch across decades of American religious and political life. He maintained a firm stance on the gospel being an inherently spiritual matter, deeply felt, and personal, rather than the gospel taking on flesh and moving into the neighborhood. This kind of faith was easy to tout in public as a way to gain favor and power but did not require a person to challenge the hierarchies established by society, and presumably by their own personal Jesus, living in their heart.

THE BIBLE SAYS . . .

It comes as no surprise to most people that the Bible has a lot to say about money, but *what* exactly the Bible says may surprise some. To understand what the Bible has to say about our finances, it is imperative to first understand the ways our current world differs from the world of the authors of the Bible.

The authors of both the Hebrew Scriptures and the Christian Scriptures wrote from within economic systems driven by agriculture. When we're reading Scripture trying to discern how to be faithful with our finances, it is an oversight to only look for passages explicitly about money. To attend faithfully to the context of Scripture, we must also consider passages about land, crops, and harvests, something that people living in agrarian economies would have known instinctively.

We must also be aware that our own economic system is not value-neutral. There are costs and benefits to all ways of organizing resources and managing money. Most Americans grow up in, and are accustomed to, a version of free-market capitalism, which is very different from the agricultural economy of the Israelites in the Hebrew Scriptures. It is important to note the different ways our economics have formed us. Capitalism, in part, emerged from the work ethic and Protestant value of simplicity. A system that demands productivity and profit as the ultimate goal, though, quickly finds itself at odds with biblical ideas of rest, Sabbath, and Jubilee. When we approach the Bible seeking wisdom about what to do with money and resources, we must take into account the differences in cultural assumptions about how money and resources are acquired. Let's look at four ways Scripture talks about this.

The tithe

Perhaps the most commonly known teaching about money in the Bible in Protestant Christian circles is the tithe. Upwards of 80 percent of Protestant Christians in the United States understand tithing as a biblical mandate for Christians today, but only around 50 percent actually give 10 percent of their income to the church or a Christian ministry.[15]

The practice of tithing is outlined in three main places in the Hebrew Scriptures. In each instance, the people are told that a tenth of their grain, fruit, seeds, and flocks belong to God. These resources provide for Israel's priests—the Levites—who were not given a plot of land to till and work (Numbers 18). The prophets Amos and Malachi both identify Israel's failure to tithe as part of why the people are in exile.

In the Christian Scriptures, bringing a tenth of a harvest is referenced in the gospels of Matthew and Luke in dialogues, but is not commanded—or even recommended—by Jesus. Otherwise, tithing is only mentioned as illustrative of the offering or sacrifice of Christ in his life, death, and resurrection.

Because members of the early church, including the authors of the Christian Scriptures, saw themselves as a part of a stream within Judaism rather than as belonging to a separate religion, it is fair to assume that they adopted some form of the command on tithing. Another approach, reflected in the early chapters of Acts, is that members of the early church gave whatever they had to ensure that no one in their midst went without (Acts 2:42-47).

Debt

Debt was a major reality in the ancient world, as it is now. The Hebrew Scriptures have multiple guidelines for what is and is not okay to hold as collateral for debt, and to whom it is okay to lend. The Israelites were prohibited from taking millstones as pledge, for example, because this would impede the indebted person's ability to earn a livelihood (Deuteronomy 24:6). Collecting interest on a loan was also forbidden (Deuteronomy 23:19).

The ideal practice for addressing indebtedness in the Hebrew Scriptures is for a family member to redeem the property for the value of the debt rather than force the indebted person to lease or sell their property. When a family member was unable to redeem the land of the indebted person, the land was leased or sold to a creditor. Even in that less-than-ideal circumstance, though, the institution of Jubilee made provision for all property to be returned to the original owners and for all debts to be canceled every fifty years (this is discussed more further on).

If the indebted person came into the means to repay their debt before the Jubilee year, they were permitted to do so and thereby redeem their own land. Leviticus 25:23-24 forbids land, a key financial resource, from being sold in perpetuity because ultimately the land belongs to God. As such, all "sales" of land—for indebtedness or other reasons—were understood only as leases. In short, the approach to debt in the Hebrew Scriptures was to require only the payment—not interest— and to do so in a way that did not inhibit the indebted person's livelihood to a significant degree. Maintaining human dignity was at the center of the ethic on debt.

Sabbath

As with the tithe, Sabbath is also widely recognized today even if it is not widely practiced. Noted in multiple places in the Hebrew Scriptures, the command to observe a Sabbath day—a day of rest—is closely tied to how we think about faithfulness in our finances because Sabbath reorients the life of the one observing it. Rest, in this instance, "is so much more than withdrawal from labor," writes Rabbi Abraham Joshua Heschel; "it is the state in which there is no strife and no fighting, no fear and no distrust."[16] For those in the agrarian cultures of the ancient Near East, observing a day of rest in which the land was left unattended and attention was instead given to the harmony of life and the goodness of the unfolding days was a radical move.

We are not so far removed from the original audience of these texts in this way. While many of us are not concerned with tending fields or vineyards or livestock, we do face demands of work encroaching on every hour of every day. Sabbath is most closely associated with time, and how we spend our time says a lot about how and to whom we assign monetary value. Are we driven to use our days to beat fear and lack, to amass and acquire, or is time a gift? An opportunity, yes, to go about the work set before us, but for the sake of faithfulness, and for provision for ourselves and for others. Theologian Walter Brueggemann writes that the practice of Sabbath

> declares in bodily ways that we will not participate in the anxiety system that pervades our social environment. We will not be defined by busyness and by acquisitiveness and by pursuit of more, in either our economics or our personal relations or anywhere in our lives. Because our life does not consist in commodity.[17]

Perhaps Sabbath, more than any other practice, helps us reframe our understanding of faith from the acquisitional story we've been handed. Sabbath, in emphasizing the nature of life as antithetical to commodification, undermines any notion of tallying up salvation totals, or measuring success by the number of congregants in attendance. Sabbath subverts the lie of a personal Jesus who abandons us in our doubt or exhaustion, who distances himself if we haven't done enough to earn his grace. Sabbath invites us into a new reality, where connection with all things and all people is restored.

Jubilee

Jubilee is a command, outlined in Leviticus 25, to cancel all debts and restore all land to the original owners every fifty years. Such an all-encompassing debt-canceling practice was not completely unheard of in the ancient Near East, but Jubilee stands apart from other ancient debt-canceling practices because the command issued from God, not from a specific ruler or king whose will could be subverted, overturned, or recalled by the king himself.[18] The basis for this command to return land to owners and cancel debts reflects the conviction that it is God who own the land, and that God's ownership provides an unchangeable basis for a community ethic of just distribution of land. This ethic also assumes that for those who are wealthy, there is an *obligation* to care for those who have fallen on hard times. Those with means will tend the land responsibly while those who have fallen on hard times recoup their losses, but the wealthy may not continue to expand their ownership of property by exploiting the indebted. God's plans for Israel and for the land will not be derailed by "the incompetence of some and the greed of others."[19]

UNLEARNING AND RETURNING: PERSONAL

A survey in the early 2000s found that only 4 percent of Christians in the United States viewed the way they managed their finances as an act of spiritual formation.[20] This seems odd, especially given the amount of time Christians spend in the public square discussing money. From televised preachers promising economic reward to radio talk show hosts couching financial advice in Scripture, Christians talk a lot about money, but generally through the lens of how to *acquire more of it.*

The story many of us have been handed about what faithfulness to God looks like with regard to our finances goes something like this: if you work hard, aren't overwhelmingly stingy, and are smart, then God will bless you financially. When those who believe this story confront experiences of financial need or systemic income inequality, their responses range from a denial that anything economic could be systemic to blaming poor people for their financial woes. But as we've seen, this story bears little in common with what Scripture has to say about being faithful in our finances.

The impulse to tie faith and finances together is correct, although the ways in which this impulse is often worked out require significant revision. For many of us, it's difficult to reimagine what conformity to Christ looks like when it comes to personal finances. There has been so much unhelpful teaching from the church on this matter, and many of us live with the reality that simply paying our bills and working to stay up to date on our student loans or medical debt is all we can manage.

We need to expand what we think about when we say "finances" to include more than just "money." Just as land and harvest were deeply associated with the financial system of the day when the Bible was being written, what are the resources associated with our financial system today? Below are some broad principles and practices that I hope are helpful in unlearning the story that equates God's blessing with financial prosperity.

Cut the commercials

Studies estimate that the average person sees between four thousand and ten thousand advertisements each day.[21] Assuming you get eight hours of sleep each night (which, I know, is laughable), that factors out to between four to ten ads *per minute*. We are literally being sold something all day, every day, all the time, so it is no wonder many of us live with the constant feeling that what we have is never enough.

While it's impossible for most of us to avoid advertisements altogether, we can cut down on how much advertising messaging affects us by limiting our exposure. We can walk into another room or mute the television during commercial breaks. We can skip ads on YouTube videos whenever possible. We can observe and track how much time we are spending on social media websites, and then consider reducing it. We can evaluate whether our magazine and newspaper subscriptions help inform us or whether they are mostly advertisements. We can consider if it's feasible to limit trips to the store or a shopping website to once per week. Before shopping, we can make a list of the things we need and stick to only those items.

Work toward getting out of debt

There are tons of blogs, podcasts, and books that outline detailed strategies for paying down debts. (There's a list in the back of the book to get you started!) Evaluate some of the strategies with a close friend, family member, spouse, or partner to see if there's one that would work well for you. Taking small steps is better than taking no steps at all, and having someone whom you trust to help you evaluate can make the process less intimidating.

If it's not feasible for you to work toward getting out of debt right now, then consider what is needed for that to become a possibility, and ask your trusted friend or partner to help you brainstorm how to make that possible.

Get creative with sharing

Scripture consistently reflects a conviction that resources do not *belong* to individuals but are stewarded *by* them. Consider ways you can creatively share the resources you have, or ask others you trust to share resources you need. Arrange to have dinner with friends each week and switch off who provides food, or split the responsibility. If you have spare bedrooms in your home, consider renting them out at very low cost (or no cost if you're able!) to college students or trade apprentices in your community. Look into ridesharing opportunities or public transportation options in your community.

Observe a "buy nothing" month

Commit to unlearning the value of consumerism by observing a month of buying nothing. This could be for a particular type of purchase you make frequently (like clothing, takeout, or—gulp—books and coffee), or if you garden or have creative ideas about how to sustain your food supply through the month, it could be literally *nothing*.[22] So much of our identity and worth is bound up in either purchasing (having cool stuff) or productivity (spending time making money to buy aforementioned cool stuff). Choosing to buy nothing helps subvert that lie and reframe our self-worth.

Practice generosity

Write out a budget for one month, accounting for all your necessary expenses (bills, rent, food, medication), then note if you have any money left over. If so, consider giving a portion of it to your church or a charity. Or do this exercise with several friends and commit to pooling your giving for a few months to pay off one person's debt before moving on to focus on eliminating debt for the next person in the group. Keep going until every person in the group has a debt paid off.[23]

The Bible talks about tithing, which we examined earlier in this chapter. Giving exactly 10 percent of your income may or may not be a practice that is feasible within your particular financial circumstances, but living a life of generosity in ways that consistently acknowledge that we are not the owners of this world and of the resources entrusted to us is something we all can practice. Practicing personal generosity when means are few may feel challenging or scary, but inviting others whom we trust into discerning how to best steward our extra money or how to best make ends meet opens a beautiful space for community to develop.

UNLEARNING AND RETURNING: PEOPLE

Issues of debt and stewardship and how to organize people in a just manner persist to this day. Some have made the argument that Jesus, in opening his public ministry with the reading of Isaiah 61 (which mentions "the year of the Lord's favor"—presumably Jubilee), is expanding the bounds of Jubilee.[24] If this is the case, then the church is invited to exemplify Christ by joining in the declaration that we now live in "the year of the Lord's favor."

The Hebrew Scriptures outline three main practices involved in Jubilee: debt forgiveness, care for the land, and practices of land stewardship and ownership. I'll address care for the land and stewardship and ownership of the land in a later chapter, but with regard to the first aspect of Jubilee, let us consider the question, What would it look like for the church to respond to its calling to declare the good news of debt forgiveness in our own contexts today?

Canceling debt

In the mid-2010s, over 70 percent of Americans who graduated from college left school with at least $28,000 in student loan debt, adding to the total $1.5 trillion in student loan debt across the United States.[25] This financial burden drives many people to work outside their preferred field (either as a primary source of employment or as additional employment to make ends meet—attractively rebranded "the side hustle"). This burden of debt also increases personal and relational stress, and delays milestones considered for the past hundred years to be markers of adulthood—things like purchasing a home, marrying, or having a child.

In January 2019, Alfred Street Baptist Church in Alexandria, Virginia, engaged in a three-week fast to seek what God was calling their congregation to in the new year. During the fast, the congregants took up a special collection, and at the end of the fast the church discerned that the Lord was calling them to pay off the debts of thirty-four graduating seniors at Howard University. The debts paid off by Alfred Street totaled $100,000.[26]

With a total in the trillions and growing, it is difficult to imagine that U.S. student loan debt might be canceled by the church alone. However, if more congregations took up a challenge similar to the one undertaken by Alfred Street to pray and fast and take up a collection to cancel the debt of someone in need, how different might the outlook be for the many indebted U.S. college graduates?[27]

UNLEARNING AND RETURNING: PUBLIC

The public witness of evangelicals has been shaped, to a great degree, by free-market capitalism and an insistence that what is best for the success of the American economy is essentially

God's best plan for our common economic flourishing. Without diving deeply into economic theories, I would invite us to consider anew the ways in which we are invited to affirm or critique our economic system.

Resources are a gift

The practice of tithing reminds us on a personal level that the resources and money we use are a gift. We do not own them. Many of the practices of European colonizers and their descendants have been predicated on forgetting this reality, even when they continued giving! Pressing for corporate responsibility around the stewarding of resources—economic and environmental—is imperative to remembering that the *earth is not ours* and that the resources it yields are a gift for our benefit, not our exploitation. Businesses and governments have a moral responsibility to steward the wealth entrusted to them with the knowledge that it doesn't—ultimately—belong to them. When companies, corporations, and governments act in ways that exploit, devalue, and seek possession rather than stewardship of economic resources, Christians have a moral imperative to say, "This is not the way."

For example, in the early 2000s, real estate in the United States boomed. Banks and mortgage brokers engaged in high-risk practices of offering loans to people who did not have the means to repay them and who did not understand the risk they were incurring by signing the loan. Under the influence of the widespread myth known as "the American dream," millions of idealistic Americans purchased homes they could not afford. Banks broke down the mortgages into smaller loans and then sold them to financial management companies. The practice was intended to lower the institutional risk of the mortgages, but instead it led to the housing crisis and recession of 2008.[28]

In my city there was a campaign in 2015 to call into account one of the owners of the local NBA team. The basketball team owners, all of whom are very wealthy individuals, were lobbying the local government to provide tax incentives to build a new arena for their team downtown. A coalition of faith leaders and activists pushed back on this proposed use of public funding. They pushed the issue forward by asking one of the owners to be accountable for the poorly maintained rental properties he owned in Milwaukee, properties that brought him wealth but into which he did not reinvest. Rallies were held and lawn signs were placed in front of the houses in question stating "This property owned by Bucks owner" to raise awareness.[29] Ultimately, the city granted the tax incentives to the owners, but not without the activists and faith leaders raising the ethics of this financial choice in the conscience of our city.

Industry tactics aimed at taking possession of wealth at the expense of human dignity and flourishing are morally wrong. Christians have a responsibility to speak truth to the system (even if the system does not change!) and to say that this is not the way things should be. Opposing exploitative lending and business practices is one way to do this.

The other national debt

There is much conversation in the public sphere about the national debt in the United States—the amount owed by the federal government because of cumulative deficits. However, institutionally, the greatest debt the United States owes is to African Americans who were trafficked and enslaved, and to Indigenous people whose land seizure made possible the economic realities of today. Reparations are a moral imperative. In an extensive article on reparations, Ta-Nehisi Coates outlines the ways the exploitation of African Americans has formed the backbone of the American economy, from enslavement to sharecropping to predatory home loans and redlining.[30]

Coates opens his article by quoting Deuteronomy 15:12-15, which instructs the Israelites to let enslaved Israelites among them go free every seventh year. The command is not simply to set the enslaved free, though, but to compensate those who had been sold into bondage. "Thou shalt not let him go away empty" is how the King James Version, cited by Coates, renders the text. Yet the United States has done exactly that to the African Americans trafficked to our shores, and to their descendants.

Citing Jesus' encounter with Zacchaeus, professor Keri Day issues a mandate to Christians specifically to seek reparations:

> In his encounter with Zacchaeus, I want to suggest that Jesus sets forth a reparations ethic. . . . Zacchaeus is expected to give back that which he has stolen so that he can be reconciled with others and God. Reconciliation cannot occur until he has given back what he has stolen.[31]

Conversations about reparations are increasingly making their way into national politics in the United States. Calling representatives and supporting candidates who are engaged in the fight for reparations is one way of bearing public witness to the lordship of Christ with regard to our finances as a nation.

7

RULE AND SUBDUE

Connection over Consumption in Relationship with Creation

The early '90s were the golden era of Saturday morning cartoons, or at least that's how I remember it. My family didn't have cable, so my weekday after-school television viewing was confined to the wholesome, enriching content of public television rather than the excitement and hilarity of Nickelodeon actors dropping buckets of slime on people. On Saturday mornings, though, my network television–only life didn't matter. All four networks became kids-only zones for hours. And I, in my pajamas with a plateful of waffles, was there for it.

One of the popular cartoons of the era featured a team of teenage superheroes who worked together to fight ecological disasters. *Captain Planet* had an irresistibly catchy theme song, and the content—to my memory—rivaled the wholesome quality of the weekday PBS shows while still maintaining an undeniable "cool" factor. During commercial breaks, public service announcements about Arbor Day and Earth Day would roll past with catchy jingles proclaiming the importance of trees and caring for the environment.

My parents weren't keen on *Captain Planet*, though. After catching a few episodes with me, they decided it wasn't content they wanted streaming into their home. They said it was too focused on the earth, which was not eternal and would one day pass away entirely when Jesus returned. We didn't observe Earth Day, and never planted a tree on Arbor Day. The people making cartoons like *Captain Planet* were exaggerating, my parents insisted, and global warming simply wasn't happening.

In their defense, it certainly didn't seem like the earth was in any sort of peril in the small community in West Virginia where I grew up, which was literally named Green Valley. The acres of trees behind my house budded lush and green every spring without fail. The creek in front of my house was home to bullfrogs and bluegills and mallard ducks. The ecosystem, as far as I could tell, was working perfectly fine. The only pollution I knowingly encountered was the occasional soda can that would float down the creek from someone further up the holler and was easy enough to fish out with a stick and dispose of properly.

It wasn't until I was an adult and living in Milwaukee that I started to take the relationship between my faith and the created world more seriously. One winter the shifting Gulf Stream plunged the city into subzero temperatures for well over a week, forming a polar vortex that threatened frostbite within mere seconds. Runoff from businesses and homes in the city routinely closed access to beaches along Lake Michigan because of bacterial contamination. Ecologists working to restore areas of the city formerly filled by factories talked about how the soil was unusable in its current state because of all the chemicals and toxins that had leached into it from manufacturing plants. I started noticing studies about the many children in my neighborhood who developed asthma from air pollutants or faced other difficulties from being exposed to lead in their drinking water. It became increasingly clear to me that if I was going to love my neighbor as myself, I would need to consider the ways in which the land my neighbor and I lived on was being affected by our presence.

THE STORY THAT FORMS US

One of the shifts in thinking that marked the colonizing era was a movement toward a view of the earth as less mysterious and magical and more comprehensible and material. People began to understand their capacity to manipulate and predict the world in new ways,[1] which was helpful in the quest to acquire wealth and natural resources for the colonizing monarchies. A belief in the inevitability of human progress emerged as colonizers made what they perceived to be advancements in their newly founded societies on the lands they had seized. They found it difficult to hold on to the wonder of "the earth is the Lord's and all that is in it" (Psalm 24:1) while staking ground for themselves and the nations from which they hailed.

In 1967, historian Lynn White identified Christianity as bearing a "huge burden of guilt" for the unfolding ecological crisis that was breaking into the consciousness of U.S. scholars. White argued that because of the religious influence at the base of the ecological crisis, the response must be equally grounded in religion.[2]

To this end, the National Association of Evangelicals issued a statement in 1970 noting that "men who thoughtlessly killed animal life to the point of extinction a hundred years ago might not have realized the implications of their actions. Today those who thoughtlessly destroy a God-ordained balance of nature are guilty of sin against God's creation. We know better."[3]

But conversations about the environmental crisis and care for the created world didn't begin to reach evangelical dinner tables nationwide until the mid-1980s. As national news outlets covered the environmental crisis, different sectors within U.S. Christianity entered discussions on creation care as well. Evangelical bastion *Christianity Today* ran articles encouraging Christians to invest in conservation and care efforts like recycling, composting, and reducing personal waste. "The time has come for evangelicals to confront the environmental crisis," proclaimed one article from 1992.[4]

Yet by the mid-1990s, issues related to environmental concerns had all but disappeared from many evangelical circles. Apprehension about "New Age" influence in the environmentalist movement spurred some evangelicals to raise theological concerns about creation care. Others, seeking to maintain a clear compass politically, found conservationist views on the environment at odds with candidates who sought to restrict legal access to abortion or to maintain legal definitions of marriage as between a man and a woman exclusively.[5] Evangelical support for creation care waned, and remains a divisive issue in many faith communities to this day despite the overwhelming urgency of climate change.

THE BIBLE SAYS . . .

In the creation story, the first humans are given the command to rule and subdue the earth. This command, taught on its own, formed in me a skepticism toward practices like recycling, using renewable energy, or anything "green." While it's true that the literal reading of the command to "rule and sub-due" in Hebrew does mean to "subjugate" or "tread upon," when held in tension with the humans' status as image-bearers of the divine, the command for humans to conduct themselves as representatives of divine authority on this earth must be reframed. Bearing the image of God is not only a statement about the value of human life; it is a statement about the responsibility humans have to the rest of the created world.

A belief that the only human responsibility toward the earth is to "rule and subdue" ignores other parts of the Bible in which we're told, "The earth is the Lord's, and all that is in it." Our understanding is shaped by the reality that we read this text in post-agrarian societies, many of us completely removed from the delicate and complex cycles of nourishing and reaping crops from the land.

In the Hebrew Scriptures, Israel is given commands about observing Sabbath years and gleaning, both of which are practices that are helpful economically and ecologically, categories that likely would not have been distinct to the authors. Repeatedly throughout the Hebrew Scriptures, readers are reminded that the earth and everything in it is the Lord's. Humanity has been entrusted as stewards, as the ones who bear the "image and likeness" of God on this earth, but we are not free to do whatever we want, because we are stewards—not owners.

Some of the challenges of investing in ecological stewardship for Christians spring from a misreading of the apocalyptic book of Revelation. Revelation, often credited to the apostle John, is written as a polemic against the Roman Empire. In Revelation, as well as in apocalyptic passages in the Hebrew Scriptures, there are violent images of what seems, on a cursory reading, to be the destruction of the earth. In these images, the sea ceases to exist, the moon turns to blood, and the sun goes dark. But is it God's plan at the end of all things to destroy the world that God declared so good in the beginning? I don't think so. God's justice is always restorative and transformative, not consumptive. God's justice takes what is corrupt or broken and makes it new but does not extract revenge or payment for the sake of God's gratification.

Revelation as a whole bears witness to such a vision for justice. The author sees "a new heaven and a new earth" coming into view, even as the "first heaven and the first earth" pass away (21:1). As biblical scholar J. Richard Middleton points out, when Paul writes about new creation coming, he does not assume the death or annihilation of a person who is now in Christ, but rather presents a different way of being within the newly understood reality.[6] An assumption that in order for something new to emerge there must be a violent destruction of the old is a reflection more of our own captivated imaginations than of the intent of the biblical authors.

UNLEARNING AND RETURNING: PERSONAL

I have so much room to grow in the area of bearing witness to the kingdom of God in caring for creation. I take small steps like recycling the paper, glass, and select plastic products our city processes, and sorting any textile waste into a bin to drop off at a local textile recycling center. Our family partners with a farm through a community-supported agriculture (CSA) program so we can eat locally grown food, resulting in a smaller impact in terms of both transportation and packaging. We purchase our clothing secondhand whenever possible, and when we must choose new (I'm not ready to commit to thrift-shop underwear yet), we purchase from companies committed to economic sustainability. These options are more expensive, so we purchase new items very infrequently.

My housemate Brianna has taught me so much about what it looks like to embrace care for the earth as part of my discipleship. Her commitment to sharing everything in our house from rides to waffle irons inspires me to think more consistently about asking to share rather than needing to own.

Domination is not discipleship
Brianna Sas-Pérez

As a child I remember riding around—to church, the grocery store, Grandma's house, anywhere—as my dad drove. Often before we'd reach the destination, and especially when we were on the highway, he would brake suddenly, pull over, and begin driving in reverse. In my earlier years I would sit up and look around, thinking at first that the car was breaking down or we were getting pulled over. Eventually I would realize that my dad had seen something on the side of the road that he deemed as still having life and purpose. This became a ritual, and whenever my siblings and I would feel the brakes, we'd groan, "¿Ahora que?" (Now what?). I remember stopping for everything from a rubber bungee cord to a car bumper; my dad always would reuse what he found. This habit seemed weird at the time, but I later realized that it had taught me to be resourceful and to create less waste. These unexpected interruptions, among many other memories, are part of what has led me to believe that caring for the earth and our resources is part of my discipleship as a follower of Jesus.

Foundational to this aspect of discipleship is the belief that God is in all things, God created all things, and as Job suggested, we can learn from the earth. I don't always experience or pay attention to this connection. That is why it is a discipline for me to practice sensing the presence of God in the world around me. Sometimes I pause to listen for birds chirping or leaves rustling amid the sounds of the ice cream truck bell ringing and basketballs bouncing; sometimes I touch my skin to feel the heat radiating from the sun and remember that the light brings literal health to my body. These practices remind me that God has created the plants that cure ailments and the air that fills our lungs.

Grounded in the belief that our connection to the earth matters (our lives are dust to dust), I have encountered another discipline: remembering that domination is not discipleship. Domination of the environment, such as contaminating the earth or misusing resources, is often part of amassing money and power. A desire to acquire or consume is often driven by a pursuit of my own comfort—driving a car (it's too far!), getting an item for myself (sharing is inconvenient!), and leaving water running during my shower (I'll be cold!) are just a few examples. My experience of privilege, which includes holding U.S. citizenship and middle-class status among much else, has inherently taught me that I can seek more for myself, that I don't have to put in extra effort, and that I can buy and discard as I please, all because I am in charge. It is an ongoing practice for me to remember that these lies of dominance harm our natural world and oppress the people who inhabit it.

More than anything else, it is a discipline for me to continually think of my neighbor first. Caring for my neighbor means caring for the neighbor who mines the metals for my cell phone, who has lead in their water, and who is affected by the deforestation of land in South America to provide grazing land to meet the United States' demand for beef. It took me years to recognize all of these groups of people as my neighbors, and I am continually learning how damage to the earth and its resources always affects people, even if it doesn't affect me directly. Folks everywhere who experience racism and poverty bear a disproportionate environmental burden because environmental injustices are layered upon other forms of oppression. Because of this, as a Christian, I have come to see that loving my neighbor means considering my impact on the environment as a pursuit of economic, racial, and other forms of justice.

Practicing these rituals, similar to my dad's ritual of giving new life to "junk," costs me time or comfort, but I'm continuing to learn the cost of not practicing them. As I seek to conform my life to Christ and to resist sins of selfishness, apathy, pride, greed, laziness, and abuse of power, these disciplines continue to help me along the way.

UNLEARNING AND RETURNING: PEOPLE

Our shared life as the people of God also affords us opportunities to engage our imaginations in ways that steward rather than consume the earth's resources. Some are super simple but require intention.

We can swap out disposable cups for mugs and avoid using a coffee-pod system to brew beverages at gatherings (or at the very least use a reusable pod and fill it with grounds). We can switch out paper products for community meals with reusable plates, cups, and flatware. This doesn't mean we have to purchase trendy, matching dishes. Local thrift stores often have mismatched plates and flatware available very inexpensively. Our congregation made this shift a couple of years ago, in addition to lessening our waste. The investment in reusable plates and flatware has paid for itself.

Check to see if your community offers compost pick-up for businesses or organizations, and if so, keep a separate bin for food waste after community meals. Check with local grocery stores to see if they have a program for distributing excess food, and consider starting a program to distribute this food to people in need. Each week our congregation receives surplus baked goods from a local grocer, and we distribute them to people who drop in looking for food. We also partner with a food rescue program to provide meals for our after-school and youth programming.

If your congregation is looking to take more drastic measures, and you have the space and the resources to try it, consider making renovations to the building you meet in to make it more ecologically friendly. In Milwaukee, Tippecanoe Presbyterian Church is an example of one congregation that has taken drastic steps to make their physical meeting space a place that provides care and stewardship to the earth instead of consumption and domination.

I visited Tippecanoe Presbyterian (also known as Tippe) one sunny July afternoon and spoke with Pastor Karen in the garden next to their outdoor labyrinth. This small church, tucked away in one of the neighborhoods on the southside of Milwaukee, is a little oasis of beauty and life—as the church should be. Here's what she shared with me when I asked about how Tippe approaches gardening in and with their neighborhood, ecological stewardship, and resisting consumeristic faith:

> We had an opportunity during the winter months to open our doors to those who are homeless, without being a formal shelter, as long as we were holding prayer vigils. Ten seasons ago, now, we started our overnight prayer vigil warming room, which is now a staple in the county.
>
> The same year we started our overnight prayer vigils, we got wind of the Victory Garden movement. It was brand new, and we started Victory Garden in our yard [at the church building]. It was very successful—so successful that many of the people who volunteered in the gardens put beds in their own yards at home—but then we started to think about how we could do things differently. That's when Divine Intervention [a ministry to those experiencing homelessness] wedded with our gardens.

[We thought,] what if we turn this into a 'just good food' garden? Justice, good for you, food. Three interns who were moving out of homelessness worked with a master gardener to move four thousand pounds of organic produce last summer. The beds wrap all the way around the church building and [are] on the rooftop as well. We have two giving gardens to share with whoever in the neighborhood wants to pick from them, and we have an underground cistern which catches the water off the roof, and we use that to water the gardens. Every week the interns take the produce to a food pantry at a local shelter, and they set up a taste testing. They make a dish and provide a recipe and let people taste the recipe and then take the veggies they need home.

The way you do anything is the way you do everything. . . . Ecology is everything, because it's ecology of spirit, presence, the earth, emotion, intellect. Everything is everything. Everything belongs. Everything we do affects everybody else, *everybody* else.

We're a forty-five-member congregation, but it's about a spirit, a spirit to do, and to collaborate and to figure it out, and to not feel like we have to drive everything. . . . If you notice, none of our ministries say "Tippecanoe Presbyterian Church" in the name, because it's not about this church. Churches have to get over the silo effect and feeling [that] they have to design and own everything. It's really hard, though. These ministries don't belong to this church. We couldn't do any of this by ourselves.[7]

Finding ways to creatively steward the resources available to your community or congregation will take time, as well as assessment of the resources you have access to. But whether it's ditching coffee pods in the church lounge or planting a garden on your roof, there is an invitation for all of us.

UNLEARNING AND RETURNING: PUBLIC

As I write this book, Wisconsin is ending one of its wettest springs on record, with a rainfall three inches more than average for this time of year. A farmer who lives about an hour away from my home in Milwaukee only has about a tenth of his crops for the year planted, a financially devastating consequence of an extraordinarily wet spring.[8]

The rain-induced plight of farmers is not limited to Wisconsin, though. Throughout the Midwest, farmers are struggling to get crops in the ground, or to salvage what has been planted from rising floodwaters. In 2016 the U.S. Environmental Protection Agency reported that in the past hundred years, annual rainfall levels had risen 20 percent in the Midwest because of climate change, with precipitation rates projected to continue to rise over the next century.[9]

With the climate crisis we're facing today, perhaps the most needed response is in the form of public witness. While personal and small community steps certainly help, larger systemic change must be made to effect the change needed to mitigate the effects of the shifting climate on planet Earth. Encourage your elected officials to support legislation that promotes renewable or sustainable energy sources and protects natural resources—like water supplies, forests, and clean air. On a local level, press for more access to public transportation, which helps lessen carbon emissions by reducing the number of cars on the road.

To curb the effects of climate change, efforts toward reducing carbon emissions have been suggested for the past twenty years, with governments around the world taking serious measures only beginning in 2015 with the signing of the Paris Agreement. Churches can help advocate "rest for the land"

(Leviticus 25:24-25) by encouraging congregants to express their support for the Paris Agreement.

A final way to get involved in bearing public witness is to join a FridaysForFuture climate strike. Swedish activist Greta Thunberg launched the weekly strike in 2018, and it has now grown into a student-led global movement. In the week I am writing this, there are nearly two thousand strikes planned for Friday on every continent. You can use the FridaysForFuture website to find out if there's a strike near you or to access resources to help you organize one. (Adults are welcome to organize too.)

8

I DO NOT PERMIT A WOMAN

Connection over Consumption in Relationship to Gender

I love routine. Every morning for a couple of years my morning routine went something like this: Wake up. Brew coffee. Spend time in prayer. Read the news. Depending on the headlines, write either an angry or encouraging journal entry or blog post.

In 2017, reading a headline with the name of a prominent man facing allegations of sexual assault, harassment, or rape became a devastating part of that routine. Survivors of these acts of violence spoke up from every sector of public life using #MeToo as their rallying cry.[1] Survivors of abuse and misconduct from within the church added their own twist to the already viral social media movement, adding #ChurchToo and dispelling any illusion that Christians aren't capable of committing such horrors.[2] As the months of 2018 ticked away, the Me Too and Church Too movements showed no signs of slowing. One thing became abundantly clear: getting saved does not magically transform a person into a respecter of the dignity and autonomy of others—and especially not of women.

I was angry and not surprised. I have always had the spirit of a leader and an entrepreneur, a spirit that often, in my growing-up years, got me labeled a "Jezebel." When it came to matters of faith, I quickly internalized the conclusion that these impulses to create and dream and lead were problems, not gifts. I prayed for hours that God would give me the "gentle and quiet spirit" that good Christian girls were supposed to have. Yet my big ideas, opinions, and dreams continually disrupted my attempts to become quiet and serene.

The waves of #MeToo and #ChurchToo survivor accounts resurrected familiar feelings in my body. Prickling shivers rushed from head to toe and twisted my belly into knots. They were as familiar as the pounding of my heartbeat that I remember from my years as a middle schooler and high schooler, when church leaders would pull me aside on a regular basis to tell me that I was causing boys to stumble or that I was being "too much." I didn't know at the time how to name those feelings as shame and a response to manipulation. Instead, I accepted the responsibility of protecting the boys around me from temptation and tried to shrink myself to fit the ideals presented to me.

I feverishly wrote out a personal list of dos and don'ts for my wardrobe in my journal. I learned to hate my body. I convinced myself that policing it was a form of love. I learned to hate my voice, to see my brains and ambition as a liability. I knew that no amount of praying and asking friends to hold me accountable was going to produce the "gentle and quiet spirit" that a true woman of God should possess. But if I disparaged myself as I spoke up, perhaps I would at least signal that I was trying.

The Me Too and Church Too movements highlight the extreme, hierarchical positions on sex and gender espoused by Christians in the United States in recent decades. These views often function to turn women into objects to consume. They constantly define women by their relationship to others as someone's wife, mother, or daughter.

To tell a different story about gender, we not only need to call into account those who abuse and exploit. We also need to challenge the distribution of power in our church and public structures to ensure that one gender does not objectify the other. I grew up believing "feminist" was antithetical to "Christian," but this isn't the only way to think about such matters.

THE STORY THAT FORMS US

Women have been involved in shaping the political and religious landscape of the United States from the beginning. Harriet Tubman and Sojourner Truth, among others, were fierce advocates for women's rights as early as the 1800s. Truth's speech "Ain't I a Woman?" brought together her faith and her fight for equity as a Black woman in the hostile years leading up to the Civil War.

> The Lady has spoken about Jesus, how he never spurned woman from him, and she was right. When Lazarus died, Mary and Martha came to him with faith and love and besought him to raise their brother. And Jesus wept—and Lazarus came forth. And how came Jesus into the world? Through God who created him and woman who bore him. Man, where is your part?[3]

World War II ushered in the earliest stages of a second wave of feminism by sending women into the workforce in unprecedented ways. The massive pool of men pulled into the armed forces left manufacturing and management jobs vacant and needing to be filled by the women on the home front. While rates of employment among American women dropped immediately after the war, women continued to enter the workforce in the decades that followed, while most men persisted in dismissing domestic labor and responsibilities.[4]

In 1973 the writers of the Chicago Declaration, a statement which marked the launch of Evangelicals for Social Action, not only lamented injustice perpetuated on the grounds of race, but also turned an eye to the inequality of women and men.[5] The Evangelical Women's Caucus, an organization that grew out of the ESA, evaluated the embedded gender hierarchies in the church and began to challenge assumptions about the role of women in church leadership.[6]

The reaction from those who disagreed was swift and decisive. Billy Graham lamented that "too many women" were "wearing the trousers in the family" as second-wave feminism rose in influence.[7] Along with his version of the gospel, Graham began proclaiming extrabiblical teachings about the role of a wife. "The Bible teaches that the wife is to make the home as happy as possible . . . as near like heaven as possible," Graham preached.[8] Rather than a vision of mutuality between men and women in stewarding what God has entrusted, as Scripture portrays, Graham focused on heavenly mansions in the sky and instructed wives to help acquire and tend to their own mansions in the here and now.

Alongside Graham's condemnation from the pulpit, evangelicals who objected to the Chicago Declaration fired back by convening their own conference and issuing the Danvers

Statement, affirming what they called "biblical manhood and womanhood."[9] Shortly after the Danvers Statement was issued, the Southern Baptist Convention, the largest evangelical denomination in the United States, rolled back policies allowing the ordination of women.[10] At the same time, the SBC shifted its benchmark for theological orthodoxy from affirmation of the doctrine of biblical inerrancy, a doctrine enshrined in the essay series *The Fundamentals* a century before, to affirmation of gender exclusivity and hierarchy.[11]

THE BIBLE SAYS . . .

In the creation narrative, the author of Genesis records that God created humanity, male and female, in the image and likeness of God (Genesis 1:26). In the ancient Near East it was common for a nation to erect a statue of its ruler or deity to mark the entrance to their territory—the "image and likeness" of their god or monarch. The author of Genesis notes that statues or idols don't mark the boundaries of the terrain under God's authority. Rather, all humanity serves as the image and likeness of God. From the beginning, *all humanity* is given the task of exercising authority and stewarding it in ways that align with the way God reigns over the world. The vision of Scripture is not that one person would hoard power and resources and lord them over others, but that all would be stewarded and shared in mutual submission.[12]

Genesis 2 (NIV) records that the woman is taken "from the side" of the man to be a "suitable helper" for him. The power of these words has often been obscured in many Christian circles. The word for the "side" from which the woman was taken is the same as the word used to refer to the sides of the ark of the covenant. It's a word used for equal opposing sides that work together to make something strong and steady. The

phrase "suitable helper" used to describe the woman, tragi-
cally translated by the King James Version as "help meet," is
used elsewhere in Scripture to refer to military reinforcements
in battle or to refer to God directly as a divine helper.

Throughout the remainder of the Hebrew Scriptures, we
are given glimpses of God's affirmation and love for women
even though the authors of the text were living within a patriarchal culture. In Exodus, it is the midwives Shiphrah and
Puah who first subvert the pharaoh by refusing to kill Hebrew
infants (1:15-20). Moses's mother and sister and Pharaoh's
daughter all play a part in rescuing and raising the child who
would grow up to deliver Israel from enslavement in Egypt
(2:1-10). In Judges 4–5, Deborah is depicted as a wise and
discerning authority with whom the Lord is pleased. Ruth—a
foreigner and a woman!—acts on her conscience, following
her mother-in-law Naomi back to Bethlehem and gleaning the
fields each day to provide for them. Esther, perhaps having no
choice, plays the risky game and charms the king of Persia into
marrying her after being placed in his harem, but then uses her
status as queen to save the Jewish people from destruction.

In the Christian Scriptures, Mary not only bears the Christ
child but prophesies powerfully over the announcement
that she is with child (Luke 1:46-55). Anna the prophetess
sings for joy in the temple when the baby Jesus is presented
(Luke 2:36-38). The woman with the issue of blood not only
is healed quietly, as she had hoped, but Jesus sees her and
speaks with her in the midst of a crowd, breaking all kinds
of social mores (Mark 5:25-34). When the Samaritan woman
at the well engages Jesus in theological debate, he responds
by entrusting her with the news that he is the Messiah and
then sends her into town to share the news with everyone she
knows (John 4:1-42).

Phoebe is Paul's co-laborer, entrusted with delivering and reading the letter that we call the book of Romans to the church (Romans 16:1-2). Mary Magdalene is named as an apostle to the apostles (John 20:11-18). Dorcas, a merchant, supplied the funding for so many in need that she is brought back to life after an untimely death (Acts 9:36-42). Priscilla worked alongside her husband, Aquila, and Paul to lead a church in their community (Acts 18; Romans 16:3).

While a handful of verses have been used throughout the years to relegate women to particular roles within the church and in life, the Bible as a whole gives no such picture. The movement throughout the text is toward what the prophet Joel declared, and what Peter echoed on Pentecost: the new reality that the Spirit of God is poured out on all flesh, old and young, male and female alike (Joel 2:28-32; Acts 2:17-21). The Spirit, in her indiscriminate overflow that invites all people to participate in the work of the Lord, asks us to resist viewing one another and our relationships as something to be consumed.

UNLEARNING AND RETURNING: PERSONAL

The Me Too and Church Too movements brought to light the underbelly of a framework that objectifies women and has long been a staple in evangelical communities. I grew up hearing and believing that the greatest calling on a woman's life was to be a wife and a mother.

I bought into this lie hook, line, and sinker, getting married as soon as I graduated from college. (Literally. Our wedding was two weeks after graduation.) But a few years later, married and with a daughter of my own by the time I was twenty-four, I came face-to-face with the stark reality that I did *not* feel as though I had achieved all that God had for me

in life. Moreover, I was certain I did not want to teach my
daughter the same story that had been told to me. I didn't
want my daughter to spend her teen years fantasizing about a
relationship she might never have with a man she may or may
not yet have met. I didn't want her to respond with alarm to
any rising emotions of a growing crush, shutting them down
like a sledgehammer out of a sense of having to give serious
consideration to whether the person fit her image of marriage
material. I never wanted my daughter to be told by a youth
pastor that her body was a dangerous stumbling block to
her male peers in their pursuit of holiness, or that if she had
sex before she was married, she was no better than a piece of
chewed-up gum.

My daughter was born holding her head high (which is a
good thing, given that I've never been great with that whole
support-the-neck thing that newborns require). She was
wide-eyed from the start, charismatic to the core. I'm in awe
that such a tiny human could contain so much personality. I
couldn't then, and still cannot now, imagine looking my little
girl in the eye one day and instructing her to hold back the
gifts that are already so evident in her life. I can't imagine
telling her that somehow, by becoming less herself, God will
be glorified more.

I refuse to be okay with my daughter growing up in a world
where hundreds of thousands of women around the world
have reason to rally behind #MeToo and #ChurchToo, and
where *every* woman I know can recount at least a handful of
times they were verbally harassed or physically assaulted.

My little girl deserves a better world.

Every little girl deserves a better world.

Motherhood may have turned me into a feminist, but it is
Jesus Christ's example and the Holy Spirit's conviction that

will keep me one. And should I ever forget, I have that little girl with my nose and her father's eyes to remind me that girls and women are people too. Becoming more like Christ requires that we live into the fullness of our humanity, not deny our humanity or make ourselves smaller so we can be consumed for someone else's gratification.

My seminary theology professor Cherith Fee Nordling emphatically describes the gospel as the good news that "you get your life back." It is in my surrender to Christ and submission to the work of the Spirit in my life that I am learning to see my gifts for sharp analysis, proclivity to action, and inability to keep silent about things that matter as invitations to participate in the life of God. My femaleness is not a liability—it is intentional. The triune God delights in watching me learn to live in the fullness of who I am, no matter what cultural norms I am fulfilling or subverting.

Unlearning patriarchy has also meant coming to terms with the relative privilege I am afforded as a cisgender, heterosexual, married woman who is a mother. The marginalizing effects of patriarchy I experience as a woman are mitigated by the fact that I check "acceptable" boxes in every other category. I could navigate life with few conflicts if I chose to stay in the lane prescribed to me by patriarchal culture, and it's a lane I have access to anytime I want. I would be remiss if I attempted to write definitively about what it looks like to conform to Christ regarding gender and sexuality on a personal level. It is a gift and a benefit to listen to and hold the stories of others in a way that allows our own journeys to be shaped by them. Stories like the one lived by my friend Holly, who taught me that being married and being a mother are aspects of privilege for which I need to account.

The idolatry of marriage

Holly Stallcup

I have lived for a husband most of my life. A husband who, come to find out, may not actually exist.

Years ago, I was listening to a podcast while going for a walk. The topic of the podcast was lust, and as I listened, the pastor's framing of lust led to a lightbulb moment for me. My takeaway from the podcast was simple: to lust is to objectify another human. This takeaway expanded the definition of lust so far past the classic physical fantasies definition that I quickly realized that I had a personal on-going relationship with lust.

While I may not have been fantasizing about steamy sex with my barista, for years I had been objectifying almost every man I met. If a man's face was semi-attractive, my eyes darted to his left ring finger. Was he available to me?

That was the number one question. No need for his name, his interests, his whole self. No need to honor him as made in the image of God. Women were wives or soon-to-be wives. Men were husbands or husbands-to-be. It was objectification in its simplest form.

This is what a consumeristic Christianity had taught me—a husband was something to be found, won over, and possessed. Men were for consumption, and eventually one man would fulfill the insatiable hunger in me. Marriage is what I was made for, as a woman and as a Christian, and if I had to dehumanize a slew of men to get my ring, I would not blink twice at the collateral damage. Marriage was ultimate.

What a small view of self.

What a small view of God.

And, as I came to realize, what a small and unloving view of men.

My unlearning process of this oversimplified, harmful view of gender, marriage, and in turn, singleness is ongoing. Years of therapy have slowly torn down the heartbreaking idol of marriage that I held so closely. I didn't just desire marriage; I worshiped it, and in that worship, I was shattered over and over again.

My obsession with marriage was like blinders on a horse. There was nothing else worth seeing. I was one-dimensional, headed toward a one-dimensional destiny that I believed God had set for me. It still grieves me to write those words. In my unlearning, I have found myself—a woman worthy of so much more than one dimension, a woman whose blinder-free eyes have partaken of the goodness of God all around her, a woman whose ultimate call is nothing short of complete and utter devotion to Jesus.

While I still deeply desire marriage, my life is full now. While I hope for the "if" moment when marriage is given to me as a gift, I am no longer constrained by the "when."

In my unwanted singleness, Christ has kindly called me to return to something deeper, to a family much bigger than one made up of a husband, wife, two kids, and a dog. In understanding myself as so much more than a "wife," I've had my eyes opened to the absurdly sweet gift that is the body of Christ—a family that has room for everyone, just as they are.

Next, I want to introduce you to my friend Ben. About a year after my spouse and I moved into intentional community, Ben moved into the upper level of the duplex. Before anyone moved into the Community House, those who already lived in the duplex would sit down and discuss how we felt the prospective person would fit with our community and raise any concerns or challenges we anticipated needing to navigate. The meeting to consider whether Ben would move in started with a question that I had never before considered: "Are you comfortable living in community with a gay man?"

Ben's friendship has turned out to be one of the greatest gifts of my ten years in Milwaukee, and his faithfulness in living with fierce vulnerability in our community has dramatically shifted the way I think about how God moves in the world, and who God calls as beloved.

We belong to everyone and no one

Ben Parman

In my parents' house there are many costumes. These remnants of lavish Halloween parties, thrown by Mom and Dad before my sister Emily and I were born, became the basis of our playtime. Invariably, Emily chose a karate or military uniform, and I chose a dress, heels, and wig. She played sports and I played with Barbies. People called her a tomboy. They called me other things.

After years of defending me from the mockery, Emily gently asked whether maybe I should adjust my voice a bit. After years of comforting me at the end of days of bullying, Dad suggested a few changes in my mannerisms. After years of listening to me cry about the words that peers weaponized against me and wondering if they were right, my mom replied firmly, "You can't be gay." My family loved me very much—and the culture was sending messages that they felt obligated, if not to deliver, then to consider.

Through high school and college, I monitored my speech and gestures in public spaces, restricting them to a culturally acceptable range. When I started doing this, a male camp counselor remarked, "I knew you'd grow up!" Recently I watched a video of myself playing the role of Joseph in a Christmas production and found myself unrecognizable. It was not a performance; it was a terrified attempt to pass for a man.

Without realizing it, my ability to perform gradually morphed into a way of obtaining approval, of peeling off some of the layers of fear, disgust, and hatred that had been papier-mâchéd on me. I would accept almost any attention but was not really attracted to men who were "effeminate." Men like me.

Years later, I resumed performing when I was cast in a lead role in the play *Oleanna*. The play is a series of private meetings between a student named Carol and a professor named John that result in a claim of sexual harassment. The director and I discovered support in the text for me to portray Carol—a role that is normally given to a woman— through the lens of gender fluidity. Carol's lines drilled to the center of me: "I know what I am," "I'm bad," "[I] overcame prejudices . . . sexual, you cannot begin to imagine." One night, as I prepared for a performance by repeating the phrase "I'm not going back," a wave of emotion rose in me, crashing onstage in the most divinely protected and totally reckless catharsis.

Playing Carol in *Oleanna* was the final catalyst for my recovery. The work of recovery has required unlearning the lies that God only loves a certain kind of man and that a romantic partnership is love in its fullest expression. It has been returning to the truth that I am loved, because I am masculine and feminine, both created in God's image. Projecting and reflecting that imagery, for me, means the vocations of performance, friendship, and celibacy, all of which I hope to practice in a way that is interconnected. As my favorite nun says, "We belong to everyone and no one."

Finally, I want to introduce you to my friend Cameron. Cameron and I led worship together for several years in Milwaukee. Through Cameron's friendship and witness, I've learned to think about gender in different ways, and to examine the ways in which being faithful to the imago Dei may call us to defy the gender binary that has been constructed in Western culture.

A more beautiful and complicated masculinity
Cameron Overton

As a child, I learned that girls wore dresses and boys wore ties; girls liked Barbies and boys played sports. I didn't understand why people kept telling me that I should wear dresses and play with Barbies when I clearly wanted to wear ties and play sports. I tried to be who I was, but society kept telling me my understanding of my gender was wrong. In seventh grade, I tried desperately to fit into the gender norms I was "supposed" to obey. I wore pink, dresses, makeup, and tight clothes. I sexualized my body and tried to get the attention of boys. It felt horrible for a thousand different reasons.

Over a decade later, I was twenty-eight years old and finally coming to the realization that I am transgender. As I became more fully who I was, so many questions emerged—What is gender? What is feminine? What is masculine? As a trans man, I am fully seen for the person God created me to be. Now I have more work to do than ever before to deconstruct my understanding of gender as I explore my own gender identity: What does it mean to be a man? I do like sports and lifting weights, and I like to be bold in meetings, but I know now that these preferences do not define what it means to be a man.

I have moved in the world, first perceived as a woman, and now as a man. It is distressingly clear that people take me more seriously when I talk now because they know I am a man. They respond by giving me more respect than they did when they saw me as a woman. It is also clear that people are more guarded around me for fear that I might be violent, something that never happened when people thought I was a woman. These cultural frameworks of toxic masculinity and gender essentialism make it so difficult to construct a loving and just view of myself and others.

I went through a time when I was desperately trying to "be a man" in a socially constructed and fundamentally unhealthy way. But when I look to Jesus as a model of manhood and masculinity, I see a beautiful mix of virtues that we've been taught to separate: kindness, nurture, power, authority, and intimacy. This is the type of healthy relationship to self and others I want to emulate. This man, Jesus, is not exclusively what we culturally see as what is "manly." Jesus does masculinity and gender in a much more beautiful and complicated way.

What if beauty lies in the expansiveness of gender, and not in the narrowness of the gender binary? Scripture tells us that God made the day and separated it from the night, yet we speak as though night and day are wholly opposite and apart from one another. But this polarity does such a disservice to God's creation. Have we forgotten about the sunset and sunrise, which bleed so beautifully from day to night and back again?

God is calling us into the expansive love of Christ. That love invites us to deconstruct toxic norms, and to live into the fullness of who we are. When we do this, we see the beauty in the sunset and the sunrise and say wow! Look what God has made—it is very good.

UNLEARNING AND RETURNING: PEOPLE
Authority, abuse, and restoring health and solidarity to the body of Christ

The first wave of feminism was spearheaded largely by women of faith. Subsequent movements for women's equality have been met with opposition by communities of faith due in part to the alliance between the leaders of early evangelicalism and corporate America, which had a vested interest in returning World War II veterans to their former jobs.

Yet in the wake of the Me Too and Church Too movements, it is abundantly clear that the church sorely needs to revisit the ways we have been assessing who is and is not fit for leadership. Matthew 18, a passage that provides wisdom for confrontation and reconciliation work, contains great wisdom in light of the ongoing accusations and unfolding revelations of misconduct in both the world and the church.

Matthew 18 begins with Jesus centering his attention on a child, an act that communicates that the most vulnerable or dependent in the community are counted as the greatest in the kingdom of God. The instruction that Jesus lays out in the rest of the chapter for addressing conflict assumes that conflictual situations will be navigated in light of this rejection of traditional power structures. When navigating conflict, it is the most vulnerable who must be centered in the conversation. Those who have traditionally held power or dominance in a community are called to move to the side, like the disciples being called to make room for the child.

Later in the chapter, Jesus evokes startling imagery of cutting off hands and plucking out eyes to avoid sinning against one's brother or sister. This gruesome imagery appears somewhat unexpectedly amid conversations about resolving conflict. Rather than giving readers a literal command to cut off limbs and gouge out eyes, this passage points to the extreme measures that followers of Jesus are commanded to take to prevent harming others. While the command is directed at the individual, it is given not for the *sake of* the individual alone but for the shared life of the community.[13]

The church father Chromatius read this pair of commands as an indictment against unfaithful priests—the "hands" and "eyes"—who seek their own greatness rather than service of the believing community or who are inattentive to their own formation within the church. In the community of believers, there will be no space for those who seek their own power or prestige at the cost of another in the community.[14] Humans are not to be turned into objects for consumption—no matter what the cause. If a pastor, deacon, or any other prominent leader within the community desires their own elevation of status, the solution Jesus poses is to cut the leader off and throw them out.

Intentionally or not, many congregations and some entire denominations have adopted metrics for success from corporate America—looking to numbers of people in attendance and church budget figures as markers for success. With the adoption of corporate values often comes a corporate model for leadership. Pastors and lay leaders are assessed on their ability to perform where the metrics matter—in their ability to increase attendance and budget—while accountability structures are established from the top down. The mutuality and discernment described by the evangelist to the community in Matthew 18 is virtually nonexistent in many church structures, and even for those who practice discernment with this understanding in mind, the work is hard and fraught. The words of the church father Chromatius to leaders concerned with their self-importance (or in our context, their 401(k)s) at the expense of others ring out with just as much challenge and truth today as ever.

The body of Christ is called, at this moment in history, equally to the prophetic opportunity of calling into account the men who have committed crimes and abuses *and also* to imagining a restorative or transformative justice practice which would allow for the work of healing on both the part of the survivor and the perpetrator. It is of utmost importance to maintain this tension, however, and not rush to attempting a restorative justice practice before allowing the grief to be aired and properly reported and for the survivor to be in a safe and protective space physically and emotionally. In considering the role of the church in responding to sexual harassment, assault, and abuse, it is paramount to center and heed the witness and wisdom of survivors in order to move forward well. I am grateful for my friend Terri for sharing her experience and insight, and the ways she helps me think through such matters.

"Am I safe here?" Considerations for the church in light of #ChurchToo

Terri Fullerton

Why do Christians care more about the crimes and oppression halfway around the world than that in American churches? One of the painful responses is something culture at large accepts, and something the church is slow to admit. Church leaders have not just made foolish decisions. They have not just engaged in immoral behavior. They are not just caught in sin. They are engaging in criminal activity.

As they heal, victims wonder why churches allow wolves dressed as sheep to prey on the vulnerable, the ones who are too young or powerless to see the perpetrator's deception and evil. Those who are targeted for abuse are often too isolated and too weak to know who to turn to for help.

Am I safe here?

Are the children safe here?

How will the leaders handle disclosure of sexual abuse in this church?

Will they believe the innocent or side with the perpetrator?

Do church leaders see the movement to address sexual abuse as one that will fade with the next big hashtag? Or will church leaders see it as an invitation to join God in seeking a path of restoration? Will church leaders participate in the restorative work of justice, or will they continue to stand in silence because the topic is uncomfortable?

The strong draw toward embracing what is comfortable has sometimes led congregations to applaud a pastor who confesses publicly that he has taken sexual advantage of a minor in the youth group, affirming his transparency and apparent repentance but failing to address the terrible harm he has perpetrated. This preference for comfort has pulled the people of God to choose a thirty-second-commercial salvation narrative over honesty about sexual abuse and misconduct. We want a polished version of restoration at the expense of truth.

Victims of sexual abuse wonder why the very people who are called to be the people of God and who say they seek restorative justice are instead siding with the powerful, the perpetrators, and the privileged. Why? Because reputation is more important than the soul-shattering pain they have inflicted. Perhaps the perpetrator is financially supportive and the church doesn't want to lose the money. Maybe it goes deeper. Perhaps we have exchanged following Christ with loyalty to a leader or church brand.

Healing does not happen at the expense of truth. People risk disclosing sexual abuse because they reach a point where they can't bear it alone. If the people of God saw how these violations decimate trust, they would understand how difficult it is for survivors to disclose the experiences that caused their trauma, especially if the abuse involved someone from church. If the victim doesn't trust you because you are a church leader, please don't take it personally. Victims are on a lifelong journey of rebuilding trust and learning to discern who is trustworthy.

The response of the people of God is crucial in this journey.

The vast majority of victims are telling the truth. A nationwide review of cases in the United States has shown that unfounded reports represent only between 2 and 10 percent of all sexual assault reports, and meanwhile, over 60 percent of cases are never reported.[15] Many victims have been told by their perpetrator that no one will believe them, and this is one of their greatest fears. Victims risk disclosing the abuse because they are searching for answers that they often are not able to articulate yet.

Does the evil that the perpetrator inflicted on me matter?

Does my pain matter? Will it ever get easier?

Does the pain matter to God?

Do I matter to God?

The people of God conform to Christ when they reveal how Jesus would and does answer these questions. People who have experienced sexual abuse have learned that words like love and trust, words that were used against them in the deepest betrayal, have little meaning. As a result, when church leaders use these same words to talk to survivors about God's love for them, the survivors may not believe them.

Love and trust, courage and vulnerability have to be relearned by survivors of abuse. This is why community is such an important part of healing for survivors of abuse.

Trust is relearned by experiencing loving actions over time by others who truly care. The church needs to pursue restorative justice and reconciliation, but not at the expense of truth. The darkness must be brought out into the light for true healing to be witnessed by all.

Expanding our vision of family

There is an additional opportunity for the church as we seek to bear witness in the face of our failure to love and protect one another as the people of God. The latest Gallup polls reveal that over 85 percent of people who identify as LGBTQ grew up in a faith community, and that 54 percent of those who grew up in a faith community have chosen to leave it, largely because they felt unloved by their congregations.[16]

As we consider the unlearning and returning that churches are invited to seek in order to be conformed to Christ and to choose connection over consumption, repenting of our homophobia and the physical and psychological toll it has wrought on the LGBTQ community—many of whom grew up in our pews—is of utmost importance. The consumer vision of Christianity handed to us over the years has idolized the nuclear family, which reinforces heteronormativity. But the idea of the nuclear family is not a biblical one. Jesus invites us to consider all who do the work of bringing about God's kingdom here on earth as it is in heaven to be our siblings (Matthew 12:48–50).

The LGBTQ community is especially wise in helping us learn what it means to expand our vision of family toward what Jesus invites us to—chosen commitment to one another that defies and transcends the bonds of biology and blood. When we exclude our LGBTQ siblings from fellowship and bar them from our pulpits, we miss the deep wisdom of their lived experience, and the work of the Holy Spirit in and through them.

UNLEARNING AND RETURNING: PUBLIC

The first wave of feminism in the late 1800s and early 1900s was deeply informed by the Christian faith and organized largely through church networks. There are significant problems with some of the organizing principles from the early feminist movement, most notably in its explicit racism and the anti-Blackness of prominent suffragettes like Susan B. Anthony,[17] yet we can still look to the model of church-based mobilization as a way of bearing public witness for gender equality. Here are some ways to consider doing so today.

Push to ratify and enact the Equal Rights Amendment

The Equal Rights Amendment was first proposed in 1923 as the Lucretia Mott Amendment. The original text was updated in 1943 by activist Alice Paul. The ERA, if ratified, would add a statement to the U.S. Constitution that "Equality of rights under the law shall not be denied or abridged by the United States or by any state on account of sex." The ERA was passed by Congress in 1972, almost thirty years after Paul's revisions. Congress originally gave states seven years to ratify the amendment, a deadline later extended to ten years. In 2020, Virginia became the thirty-eighth state to ratify the ERA, but it has still not been added to the U.S. Constitution.[18] In February 2020, the House of Representatives passed a resolution removing the deadline for ratification from the ERA. At the time of this writing, contacting your Senators to ask them to vote in favor of H.J. Res. 79 is the best way to support the enactment of the ERA.

Vote to protect and support mothers

The politicians and policies we support can have a significant effect on mothers and their families. We should look to support access to maternal healthcare, paid maternity and paternity leave, and subsidized healthcare. The United States has one of the highest rates of maternal mortality in countries of comparable economic status. The maternal mortality rate for African American women is even more abysmal—four times higher than the already unacceptably high rate of mortality for white women.[19] Among all nations of the world, at the time of this book's publication, the United States is one of only five nations that don't have mandatory paid maternity leave. (The other four are Lesotho, Liberia, Papua New Guinea, and Swaziland.) Some employees in the United States are granted twelve weeks of guaranteed nonpaid leave through the Family Medical Leave Act of 1993, but FMLA does not apply to all employment positions. For example, if someone has been employed at a job for less than twelve months, they cannot apply for FMLA leave, and businesses who employ less than fifty people are not required to provide it. This lack of access to time needed for adequate rest and recovery leading into and immediately after childbirth puts both mothers and infants at a higher risk for complications.

Christians in the United States have long been associated with political opposition to legal abortion access, but their advocacy has often failed to take into account the economic factors that lead women to seek an abortion. The primary reason women seek abortion is because they cannot afford to care for a child or another child.[20] Abortion rates are already the lowest they've ever been since *Roe v. Wade*. This drop is observed across the board, regardless of whether states have limited legal access to abortion. If we are to take seriously the words of the women seeking abortions, then it is clear that providing paid maternity leave and access to maternal healthcare is one of the best ways to continue to reduce abortion rates. To truly embody an ethic that upholds the sacredness of life, Christians must use their public witness to advocate for guaranteed paid leave and affordable or no-cost medical access for new mothers.

Push to end the backlog of untested rape kits

According to End the Backlog, a national rape and sexual violence advocacy project, hundreds of thousands of untested rape kits are sitting in police departments across the United States. On average it costs $1,000 to $1,500 to test a rape kit, but many forensics departments lack the equipment, funding, or training to make this a priority. Testing rape kits both brings perpetrators to justice and can prevent serial rapists from committing repeat crimes.

The evidence obtained from testing a rape kit can identify an unknown perpetrator or confirm the identity of a known suspect, as well as confirm the survivor's account of the attack. This evidence translates to an increase in arrests made in rape cases and the prevention of additional rapes. When New York State ended its testing backlog, arrests in cases of rape jumped from 40 percent to 70 percent. Nationally, rape suspects are arrested only 24 percent of the time. Encouraging your local or state elected officials to take action and pass policies requiring that rape kits be tested consistently and in a timely manner can help end the backlog and bring justice for survivors of rape in your community.[21]

Know the laws in your state about LGBTQ exclusion, and support a LGBTQ legal center

In thirty states it is legal for landlords to evict a tenant for their sexual orientation or gender identity. It is also legal in these states for employers to fire someone based on their sexual orientation or gender identity.[22] This places people who identify as LGBTQ in an incredibly vulnerable position, exposing them to the risk of being denied or abruptly removed from work and housing without further reason or explanation.

Find out what the laws are in your state regarding workforce and housing discrimination and urge your elected officials to support legislation that protects the rights of LGBTQ people to work and live without fear of discrimination. You can also find out if there is a legal center in your town or city that provides services to LGBTQ people facing discrimination; consider volunteering your time or contributing financially to their work.

Advocate for your state to end conversion therapy for minors

Conversion therapy, also known as "reparative therapy," attempts to change a person's sexual orientation or gender identity using hypnosis, electric shock therapy, or other forms of behavior modification. This practice has been discredited by every major medical and psychological authority and is broadly considered harmful.[23] Exodus International, a now defunct ex-gay ministry, closed its operations in 2017 and apologized for the harm done to the LGBTQ community by attempting and promoting conversion therapy.[24] Yet in many states, conversion therapy—including on minors, who cannot provide consent—is completely legal and unrestricted.

Encouraging your elected officials to end conversion therapy, especially for minors, is a way of bearing public witness to the kingdom of God. No person should endure electric shock therapy that has no therapeutic value, or other forms of "treatment" considered ineffective and harmful by medical science. This violation of human flourishing stands in direct opposition to the vision of shalom cast by the witness of Scripture.

9

CONSUMING CHRIST

What Broken Bread Teaches Me about Salvation

Communion is my favorite liturgy; it has been since I was a child. When I was young, one of the women who lived down the road would bake the communion bread fresh each month for our congregation's communion table. When the bread was served during worship, I would rip off as large a handful as I could get away with without catching a glare from one of my parents. I learned early that there was something wonderful and expectant about gathering together to remember and enact a body broken and blood poured out. I learned that the presence of Christ is lavish and good, and we experience it because someone else took the time to pave the way or bake the bread. In turn, we are invited to make way for another.

These days I am the one breaking the bread and holding it up in the midst of a gathering. This is a symbol of Christ's body broken for us, and a mystery that we partake in, reminding us that we too are Christ's body, breaking open to one another. My own daughter and the other children scurry to the front, yanking off handfuls of bread amid the adults who try to pinch off polite amounts and have forgotten that the one we are remembering instructed us to come like children. I stoop down toward the children's eager fingers, looking them in the eye and declaring over each child by name, "This is Christ's body, broken for you." Because the body is broken for all of us, and we're invited to come to the fullness of that with wide eyes and eager hands. You belong, in your particularity and in the ways that life transcends you.

Throughout this book I've invited you to consider anew what it looks like to be saved, that perhaps our conversations about Jesus as a "personal Lord and Savior" are not wrong but are decidedly incomplete. I have introduced an alternative way of thinking about what it means to be saved—a threefold understanding in which the operative word is *be*. It's a way of being in which we are also invited to act and speak and love and move. These actions are evidence of the kingdom coming in our midst, the fruit of our abiding in the love of God and then passing it on to others.

I've traced the history of evangelical faith in the United States, which for many of us has formed the story of what it means to be saved. I've invited you to reflect on the stories that have formed us so that we might better discern God's invitation as we move forward. We cannot respond to the invitation extended to us if we are determined to hold on to the stories that we have been handed as though they were God. The story that has formed our past does not have to form our future, but learning a new story will require us to be both brave and tender, critical and kind. We will need time and practice and humility. Our calling is to be like wheat that falls to the ground and breaks open, yielding new harvest, and like bread, crafted from that wheat, broken and passed around, reminding us there is new life.

Christian faith as expressed in the United States has largely been shaped by our consumer mindset, teaching us to focus on our own needs and wants: I want Jesus on my side, and in my heart. I want my bread molded into a personalized wafer, not broken and crumbly. I want my cup portioned out just for me so I don't have to share. Communities of faith have been established based on the judgment of gatekeepers who seek to ensure that everyone on the inside is alike, and to expel those who are "other." As long as we continue to be fearfully preoccupied with the differences of our neighbor, we will miss the ways in which Christ is coming to meet us in their words, their embrace, their presence. We will miss the moments in which they are passing us crumbly bread and inviting us to take and eat.

I've offered lots of suggestions for unlearning the path we've been formed to walk and to return instead to the connection and mutuality into which Christ invites us. We are invited to become like Christ's body, broken for you and me. This invitation may seem overwhelming. The center is not always clear. For many of us, we were given one or two hills to die on—one or two public concerns that were the line in the sand between belonging to the people of God and being seen as an outsider.

In reality, the only lines in the sand are being drawn by the One who refuses to condemn and refuses to judge. The line in the sand is love, but that isn't always an easy rallying cry around which to build a coalition. Love is not easily pinned down to one political party or one viewpoint in a ballot box. Love risks and hopes and falls short but still shows up, and somehow never fails even when we're sure we've fallen too far.

The question I've asked in this book is, What does it mean to be saved? In asking this question, I'm seeking to set you on a path toward living a life that is shaped by a view of salvation that is not a status to possess or a trinket to tuck in a corner on a dusty shelf. Salvation is not a membership card to carry around and use to leverage access to power and privilege.

Salvation is a way of being with God, yourself, your neighbor, and the world around you, and that means the ways of "being" extended to us in salvation move and flow and change. Salvation breaks and multiplies like bread. It pours out and splashes and leaves the places where it was stained like wine.

The antidote to the consumerism plaguing our view of salvation is a commitment to both maintain our particularities as the gifts from God that they are and simultaneously commit to a posture of self-giving love. The opposite of consumption is connection. Bread broken and passed from hand to hand. A cup poured out for me and for you, and for them too.

RECOMMENDED READING

Over the past decade I've found the mantra "Look for the faithful witness" extremely helpful when navigating my shifting faith. In addition to the many books I've cited in the notes for this book, the following are some of my favorites when looking for a different way to approach faith and praxis. Books are organized alphabetically by title.

Educating All God's Children: What Christians Can—and Should—Do to Improve Public Education for Low-Income Kids by Nicole Baker Fulgham

Everything Happens for a Reason: And Other Lies I've Loved by Kate Bowler

Exclusion and Embrace: A Theological Exploration of Identity, Otherness, and Reconciliation by Miroslav Volf

Faith-Rooted Organizing: Mobilizing the Church in Service to the World by Alexia Salvatierra and Peter Heltzel

Glorious Weakness: Discovering God in All We Lack by Alia Joy

The God Who Sees: Immigrants, the Bible, and the Journey to Belong by Karen González

I Bring the Voices of My People: A Womanist Vision for Racial Reconciliation by Chanequa Walker-Barnes

I'm Still Here: Black Dignity in a World Made for Whiteness by Austin Channing Brown

Jesus and the Disinherited by Howard Thurman

No Salvation Outside the Poor: Prophetic-Utopian Essays by Jon Sobrino

One Coin Found: How God's Love Stretches to the Margins by Emmy Kegler

Prophetic Lament: A Call for Justice in Troubling Times by Soong-Chan Rah

Reconstructing the Gospel: Finding Freedom from Slave-holder Religion by Jonathan Wilson-Hartgrove

Rescuing the Gospel from the Cowboys: A Native American Expression of the Jesus Way by Richard Twiss

Revive Us Again: Vision and Action in Moral Organizing and *The Third Reconstruction: How a Moral Movement Is Overcoming the Politics of Division and Fear* by William J. Barber II

Southern Horrors: Lynch Law in All Its Phases by Ida B. Wells

Strength to Love by Martin Luther King Jr.

The Very Good Gospel: How Everything Wrong Can Be Made Right by Lisa Sharon Harper

The View from Rock Bottom: Discovering God's Embrace in Our Pain by Stephanie Tait

RESOURCES FOR GETTING OUT OF DEBT

Talking about money is a big, loaded thing, and issues like debt are bigger than just individual choices. I recommend reading or engaging with both practical choices to think through the day-to-day and pieces that speak to economic theory and theology to help us imagine a better system moving forward. To get you started, here are a few recommendations:

Generosity Monk by Gary Hoag. Hoag has several blogs, meditations, and books available regarding generosity and stewardship.

Jubilee Baptist Church has an awesome newsletter that will spark your imagination for what could be possible if the people of God decided we were going to take seriously the

practices of debt forgiveness outlined in Scripture. You can
sign up on their website, JubileeBaptist.church.

Money and Possessions by Walter Brueggemann (from the
Interpretation: Resources for the Use of Scripture in the
Church series).

Mr. Money Mustache is a blog that is a *little* intense but has
some good resources for everything from getting out of
debt to how to make investments. Take it with a grain of
salt . . . or several grains of salt.

You Need a Budget. YNAB is an app and a book to help you
learn how to budget and how budgeting can help you
move toward a more intentional relationship with money.

NOTES

CHAPTER 1

1 Ron Sider, *Rich Christians in an Age of Hunger* (Westmont, IL: InterVarsity Press, 1984).

2 From 1 John 4:19, which I memorized in a Sunday school song as a child, but it didn't start to sink in till I heard my friend Brandon Brown say, "Before anything else we're loved" every week for a year.

CHAPTER 2

1 Mark A. Noll's *America's God: From Jonathan Edwards to Abraham Lincoln* (New York: Oxford University Press, 2002) is very helpful in fleshing out the narrative of the religious climate during the colonizing era.

2 James A. Morone, *Hellfire Nation: The Politics of Sin in American History* (New Haven: Yale University Press, 2004), 100–101.

3 Ibid., 109.

4 Noll, *America's God*, 31.

5 Morone, *Hellfire Nation*, 32.

6 Ibid., 31.

7 Quoted in Brené Brown, *Daring Greatly: How the Courage to Be Vulnerable Transforms the Way We Live, Love, Parent, and Lead* (New York: Penguin, 2015), 1.

CHAPTER 3

1 Jim Wallis, *God's Politics: A New Vision for Faith and Politics in America* (San Francisco: Harper, 2005), 31.

2 Julie Canlis, "The Bible's Best Description of Salvation Is a Phrase We Rarely Use," CT Women, January 29, 2019, https://www.christianitytoday.com/women/2019/january/bibles-best-description-salvation-is-phrase-we-rarely-use.html.

3 Catherine Mowry LaCugna, "God in Communion with Us: The Trinity," in *Freeing Theology: The Essentials of Theology in Feminist Perspective*, ed. Catherine Mowry LaCugna (San Francisco: Harper, 1993), 93.

4 Dave Fitch's religious pluralism class at Northern Seminary in fall 2018 was incredibly formational for this framework.

5 Vincent Bacote, "What Is This Life For?," in *What Does It Mean to Be Saved? Broadening Evangelical Horizons of Salvation*, ed. John G. Stackhouse Jr. (Grand Rapids, MI: Baker Academic, 2002), 99.

6 Describing faith as a "deeply felt" matter rose to popularity under President Dwight D. Eisenhower, who enlisted the help of Billy Graham to leverage Christian voters in his favor. Before this, faith as "deeply felt" and personal matter was not as pervasive.

7 My friend Brandon Brown, in almost every sermon I've heard him preach, and in most conversations we've had.

8 Gordon Fee, *Paul, the Spirit, and the People of God* (Grand Rapids, MI: Baker Academic, 1996), 64, 66. Emphasis in the original.

9 Tomáš Halík, *I Want You to Be: On the God of Love*, trans. Gerald Turner (Notre Dame, IN: University of Notre Dame Press, 2016), 8.

10 Ibid., 8.

11 Ibid., 9.

12 Wallis, *God's Politics*, 35.

13 Walter Brueggemann, *The Prophetic Imagination* (Minneapolis, Fortress Press, 1978).

14 Ida B. Wells, "Our Country's Lynching Record," *The Survey* 29, no. 18 (February 1, 1913): 573–74, quoted in James H. Cone,

The Cross and the Lynching Tree (Maryknoll, NY: Orbis Books, 2011), 131.

15 Cone, *Cross and Lynching Tree*, 127.

16 Devon W. Carbado and Don Weise, eds., *Time on Two Crosses: The Collected Writings of Bayard Rustin* (San Francisco: Cleis Press, 2015), 11.

17 Ibid., xi.

18 Please read more about the work that Carlos Rodríguez is doing at thehappygivers.com.

19 The Poor People's Campaign was established in 1968 under the leadership of King and the SCLC. In 2018, Barber and others launched the Poor People's Campaign: A National Call for a Moral Revival. Read more, and find out how to get involved in a local chapter of the campaign, at poorpeoplescampaign.org.

20 Lottie Joiner, "Bree Newsome Reflects on Taking Down South Carolina's Confederate Flag 2 Years Ago," Vox, June 27, 2017, https://www.vox.com/identities/2017/6/27/15880052/ bree-newsome-south-carolinas-confederate-flag.

CHAPTER 4

1 Matthew Avery Sutton, *American Apocalypse: A History of Modern Evangelicalism* (Cambridge, MA: The Belknap Press of Harvard University Press, 2014), 246.

2 Ibid., 35, 98.

3 Jeff Sharlet, *The Family: The Secret Fundamentalism at the Heart of American Power* (New York: Harper Perennial, 2009), 143.

4 Kevin Kruse, *One Nation Under God: How Corporate America Invented Christian America* (New York: Basic Books, 2015), 4–6.

5 Ibid., 6.

6 Ibid., 7.

7 James Fifield, "America's Future," no. 5, series 4 [May 1938], box 59, Herbert Hoover Presidential Library and Archives, West Branch, IA, quoted in Kruse, *One Nation Under God*, 12.

8 Ibram X. Kendi, *Stamped from the Beginning: A Definitive History of Racist Ideas in America* (New York: Bold Type Books, 2017), 361.

9 Sharlet, *The Family*, 197. Emphasis mine.

10 Kruse, *One Nation Under God*, 68.

11 James A. Morone, *Hellfire Nation: The Politics of Sin in American History* (New Haven: Yale University Press, 2004), 382.

12 Kruse, *One Nation Under God*, 18, 225; and Bethany Moreton, *To Serve God and Wal-Mart: The Making of Christian Free Enterprise* (Cambridge, MA: Harvard University Press, 2009), 182.

13 Martin Luther King Jr., "Beyond Vietnam," speech delivered at Riverside Church, April 4, 1967.

14 Jemar Tisby, *The Color of Compromise: The Truth about the American Church's Complicity in Racism* (Grand Rapids, MI: Zondervan, 2019), 166.

15 Morone, *Hellfire Nation*, 453.

16 Sutton, *American Apocalypse*, 254.

17 This is a major theme in several of the Prophets, perhaps most notably in Isaiah, Malachi, and Ezekiel.

18 Walter Brueggemann examines the monarchy through this lens in *The Prophetic Imagination* (Minneapolis, Fortress Press, 1978).

19 Pastor Brian Zahnd did this during the 2016 U.S. presidential election and wrote about it on his blog. See "How I'm Voting," *Brian Zahnd*, July 31, 2016, brianzahnd.com/2016/07/how-im-voting.

CHAPTER 5

1 "Economic Impact of Immigration," American Farm Bureau Federation, accessed February 6, 2020, https://www.fb.org/issues/immigration-reform/agriculture-labor-reform/economic-impact-of-immigration.

2 United Farm Workers and the National Farm Worker Ministry are both great places to read more about injustices in the agricultural industry.

3 Ibram X. Kendi gives the history of the formation of race an exhaustive treatment in his book *Stamped from the Beginning: A Definitive History of Racist Ideas in America* (New York: Bold Type Books, 2017).

4 Mark Charles and Soong-Chan Rah, *Unsettling Truths: The Ongoing Dehumanizing Legacy of the Doctrine of Discovery* (Downers Grove, IL: InterVarsity Press, 2019), 15–22.

5 "Dum Diversas," Doctrine of Discovery, last updated July 23, 2018, https://doctrineofdiscovery.org/dum-diversas/.

6 Josiah Strong, *Our Country: Its Possible Future and Its Present Crisis* (New York: Baker and Taylor, 1886), 165, 175, quoted in

Kelly Brown Douglas, *Stand Your Ground: Black Bodies and the Justice of God* (Maryknoll, NY: Orbis Books, 2015), 94. Emphasis in the original.

7 Douglas, *Stand Your Ground*, 94.

8 Mark A. Noll, *America's God From Jonathan Edwards to Abraham Lincoln* (New York: Oxford University Press, 2002), 19.

9 Quoted in Kendi, *Stamped from the Beginning*, 63, 64.

10 In *Stamped from the Beginning*, Kendi examines several instances of this, most notably the subversion of English common law forbidding Christians from enslaving one another.

11 Kendi, *Stamped from the Beginning*, 40–41.

12 Darren Dochuk, *From the Bible Belt to the Sun Belt* (New York: W. W. Norton, 2011), 83.

13 Kendi, *Stamped from the Beginning*, 349.

14 Matthew Avery Sutton, *American Apocalypse: A History of Modern Evangelicalism* (Cambridge, MA: The Belknap Press of Harvard University Press, 2014), 278.

15 Jemar Tisby, *The Color of Compromise: The Truth about the American Church's Complicity in Racism* (Grand Rapids, MI: Zondervan, 2019), 136–38.

16 Sutton, *American Apocalypse*, 330.

17 Randall Balmer, "The Real Origins of the Religious Right: They'll Tell You It Was Abortion. Sorry, the Historical Record's Clear: It Was Segregation," Politico, May 27, 2014, https://www.politico.com/magazine/story/2014/05/religious-right-real-origins-107133.

18 Michelle Alexander's book, *The New Jim Crow: Mass Incarceration in the Age of Colorblindness* (New York: The New Press, 2010), and Dominique DuBois Gilliard's *Rethinking Incarceration: Advocating for Justice That Restores* (Downers Grove, IL: IVP Books, 2018) are essential to understanding the incredible impact of mass incarceration on communities of color.

19 The entire book of Ruth. (It's only four chapters.)

20 This reading of the text is suggested as a possible interpretation by Wilda C. Gafney in *Womanist Midrash: A Reintroduction to the Women of the Torah and the Throne* (Nashville: Westminster John Knox, 2017), 212–13.

21 Gafney, *Womanist Midrash*, 221.

22 This is a paraphrase of a tweet posted by writer Ijeoma Oluo, "The beauty of anti-racism is that you don't have to pretend to be free

of racism to be an anti-racist. Anti-racism is the commitment to fight racism," Twitter, July 14, 2019, 5:38 p.m., https://twitter.com/ijeomaoluo/status/1150565193832943617.

23 Tisby, *Color of Compromise*, 107.

24 Ibid., 116.

25 Charles and Rah, in a lecture on their book *Unsettling Truths*.

26 Christena Cleveland, *Disunity in Christ: Uncovering the Hidden Forces That Keep Us Apart* (Downers Grove, IL: InterVarsity Press, 2013), 21.

27 Francisco Erwin Galicia, a U.S. citizen from Texas, was detained by ICE officials for twenty-three days during the summer of 2019.

28 Find out more about the movement for Truth and Conciliation on Charles's website, wirelesshogan.com.

29 You can read Coates's full statement on *The Atlantic*'s website, https://www.theatlantic.com/politics/archive/2019/06/ta-nehisi-coates-testimony-house-reparations-hr-40/592042.

30 This discrepancy has been discussed at length by Michelle Alexander in *The New Jim Crow*. For people or congregations seeking to address criminal justice reform through a faith-based lens, Dominique DuBois Gilliard's *Rethinking Incarceration* is an excellent resource.

CHAPTER 6

1 James A. Morone, *Hellfire Nation: The Politics of Sin in American History* (New Haven: Yale University Press, 2004), 32.

2 Ibid., 36.

3 Mark A. Noll, *America's God: From Jonathan Edwards to Abraham Lincoln* (New York: Oxford University Press, 2002), 4..

4 Steven K. Green, *Inventing a Christian America: The Myth of the Religious Founding* (Oxford University Press, 2015), 33–34.

5 Morone's *Hellfire Nation* does an excellent job tracing this thread.

6 Jemar Tisby, *The Color of Compromise: The Truth about the American Church's Complicity in Racism* (Grand Rapids, MI: Zondervan, 2019), 116.

7 John Fea, *Believe Me: The Evangelical Road to Donald Trump* (Grand Rapids, MI: Eerdmans, 2018), 112.

8 Darren Dochuk, *From the Bible Belt to the Sun Belt* (New York: W. W. Norton, 2011), 52.

9   Quoted in Matthew Avery Sutton, *American Apocalypse: A History of Modern Evangelicalism* (Cambridge, MA: The Belknap Press of Harvard University Press, 2014), 242.

10 Morone, *Hellfire Nation*, 351.

11 Ibid., 350.

12 Kevin Kruse, *One Nation Under God: How Corporate America Invented Christian America* (New York: Basic Books, 2015), 5.

13 Sutton, *American Apocalypse*, 239.

14 Quoted in Kruse, *One Nation Under God*, 53.

15 Bob Smietana, "Churchgoers Say They Tithe, but Not Always to the Church," Lifeway Research, May 10, 2018, https://lifeway research.com/2018/05/10/churchgoers-say-they-tithe-but-not-always-to-the-church/.

16 Abraham Joshua Heschel, *The Sabbath* (New York: Macmillan, 1995).

17 Walter Brueggemann, *Sabbath as Resistance: Saying No to the Culture of Now* (Louisville: Westminster John Knox, 2014), 31–32.

18 Jacob Milgrom, *Leviticus 23–27*, Anchor Bible Commentary (Yale University Press, 2001), 2167–69.

19 John Goldingay, *Exodus and Leviticus for Everyone* (Louisville: Westminster John Knox, 2010), 182.

20 David Kinnaman and Gabe Lyons, *UnChristian: What a New Generation Thinks about Christianity . . . and Why It Matters* (Ada, MI: Baker Books, 2007), 50.

21 Ron Marshall, "How Many Ads Do You See in One Day?" Red Crow Marketing, September 10, 2015, https://www.redcrow marketing.com/2015/09/10/many-ads-see-one-day/.

22 The documentary *Just Eat It: A Food Waste Story* (Vancouver, BC: Peg Leg Films, 2014) follows two filmmakers in their journey to quit grocery shopping and eat only food they can salvage. I'm not recommending we all take up dumpster diving (although my family did try it for several months a couple of years ago!), but it is a helpful look into how much food is wasted every year.

23 Circle of Hope, a church in Philadelphia, did this. You can read their story in the July 2019 issue of *Sojourners* magazine. Other congregations are experimenting with this approach as well; see the resource list for getting out of debt in the back of the book.

24 J. Richard Middleton, *A New Heaven and a New Earth: Reclaiming Biblical Eschatology* (Ada, MI: Baker Academic, 2014), 264–65.

25 Sarah Goldy-Brown, "Student Loan Debt Statistics," Student Debt Relief, last updated October 23, 2019, https://www.studentdebt relief.us/student-loans/student-debt-statistics/.

26 Morgan Smith, "'A Huge Weight Off of My Shoulders': Virginia Church Pays Howard Students' Debt," February 10, 2019, https://www.washingtonpost.com/local/education/a-huge-weight-off-of-my-shoulders-virginia-church-pays-howard-students-debt/2019/02/10/71424f42-2ae6-11e9-b011-d8500644dc98_story.html. The church also gave $50,000 to Bennet College, a women-only historically Black college. To view some of the students' responses, see Alfred Street Baptist Church, "When 4,000 People Fast and Pray," February 3, 2019, video, 6:59, https://www.youtube.com/watch?v=2kf2TKk96yk&feature=share.

27 Alfred Street is not alone in canceling debts. In addition to Circle of Hope, mentioned in note 23 of this chapter, several other churches have taken on canceling debt for people in their congregations or in the community around them. Grand Rapids First, in Wyoming, Michigan; Stetson Baptist Church of DeLand, Florida; and Fuel Church of Kokomo, Indiana, all paid off medical debt for members of the surrounding community.

28 Richard Rothstein, *The Color of Law: A Forgotten History of How Our Government Segregated America* (New York: Liveright, 2017), 190–92.

29 Don Walker, "Common Ground Calls Bucks Co-owner Edens a 'Slum-Lord,'" *Milwaukee Journal Sentinel*, January 29, 2015, http://archive.jsonline.com/news/milwaukee/common-ground-calls-bucks-co-owner-edens-a-slumlord-b99435465z1-290216331.html.

30 Ta-Nehisi Coates, "The Case for Reparations," *The Atlantic*, June 2014, https://www.theatlantic.com/magazine/archive/2014/06/the-case-for-reparations/361631/.

31 Keri Day, "The Black Manifesto: Remembering the Church's Call," sermon delivered at Riverside Church, May 5, 2019, video, 1:09:00, https://www.youtube.com/watch?v=gXHr7172Cus.

CHAPTER 7

1 Mark A. Noll, *America's God: From Jonathan Edwards to Abraham Lincoln* (New York: Oxford University Press, 2002), 4.

2 Quoted in Laurel Kearns, "Saving the Creation: Christian Environmentalism in the United States," *Sociology of Religion* 57, no. 1 (Spring 1996).

3 "Resolution: Ecology," National Association of Evangelicals, 1970, available at https://www.nae.net/ecology/.

4 Sabrina Danielsen, "Fracturing over Creation Care," *Journal for the Scientific Study of Religion* 52, no. 1 (March 2013).

5 Ibid.

6 J. Richard Middleton, *A New Heaven and a New Earth: Reclaiming Biblical Eschatology* (Ada, MI: Baker Academic, 2014), 254.

7 Special thanks to Pastor Karen for sharing Tippe's story with me.

8 Caroline Reinwald, "Rainfall Puts Wisconsin Farmers Weeks behind Schedule, Costing Them Thousands," WISN 12, May 28, 2019, https://www.wisn.com/article/rainfall-puts-wisconsin-farmers-weeks-behind-schedule-costing-them-thousands/27588117.

9 "Climate Impacts in the Midwest," US EPA, September 30, 2016, https://19january2017snapshot.epa.gov/climate-impacts/climate-impacts-midwest_.html. (As of January 19, 2017, this information was no longer available on the official EPA website; the URL links to historical material reflecting the EPA website before the change.)

CHAPTER 8

1 The Me Too movement was founded by activist Tarana Burke in 2006 to support survivors of sexual violence, Black women and girls in particular, as well as other young women of color. The hashtag went viral in 2017.

2 #ChurchToo was created by Emily Joy and Hannah Paasch on Twitter, and information about the hastag is outlined further on Emily's blog, emilyjoypoetry.com/churchtoo.

3 Marius Robinson, "Women's Rights Convention," *Anti-Slavery Bugle* (New-Lisbon, OH), June 21, 1851, 160, available at https://chroniclingamerica.loc.gov/lccn/sn83035487/1851-06-21/ed-1/seq-4/.

4 James A. Morone, *Hellfire Nation: The Politics of Sin in American History* (New Haven: Yale University Press, 2004), 178–79.

5 "Chicago Declaration of Evangelical Concern," Evangelicals for
   Social Action, November 25, 1973, https://www.evangelicals
   forsocialaction.org/about-esa-2/history/chicago-declaration-
   evangelical-social-concern/.

6 Matthew Avery Sutton, *American Apocalypse: A History of
   Modern Evangelicalism* (Cambridge, MA: The Belknap Press of
   Harvard University Press, 2014), 342.

7 Ibid., 332.

8 Ibid., 333.

9 The Danvers Statement was published by the Council on Biblical
   Manhood and Womanhood in 1988. The text is available at
   https://cbmw.org/about/danvers-statement/.

10 "Resolution on Ordination and the Role of Women in Ministry,"
   127th session of the Southern Baptist Convention, Kansas City,
   MO, June 12–14, 1984.

11 Bethany Moreton, *To Serve God and Wal-Mart: The Making of
   Christian Free Enterprise* (Cambridge, MA: Harvard University
   Press, 2009), 120.

12 Professor Cherith Fee Nordling, in her Introduction to Theology
   lectures, was the first person to connect these dots for me.

13 Fredrick Dale Bruner, *The Churchbook: Matthew 13–28*, vol. 2 of
   Matthew: A Commentary (Grand Rapids, MI: Eerdmans, 1990),
   214–15.

14 Manlio Simonetti, *Matthew 14–28*, Ancient Christian Commentary
   on Scripture: New Testament Ib (Downers Grove, IL: IVP Books,
   2002), 72.

15 National Sexual Violence Resource Center, "False Reporting"
   (Harrisburg, PA: National Sexual Violence Resource Center, 2012),
   https://www.nsvrc.org/sites/default/files/Publications_NSVRC_
   Overview_False-Reporting.pdf.

16 Andrew Marin, "A Spiritual Homecoming for LGBT People?,"
   Evangelicals for Social Action, April 10, 2019, https://www.
   evangelicalsforsocialaction.org/oriented-to-love-sexual-justice/
   spiritual-homecoming-lgbt-people/.

17 *Women, Race, and Class* by Angela Y. Davis (New York: Random
   House, 1981) is an excellent resource for examining anti-blackness
   in the suffragist movement.

18 Read more about the Equal Rights Amendment and find tools for advocating for its ratification in your state at equalrightsamendment .org.

19 Amy Roeder, "America Is Failing Its Black Mothers," *Harvard Public Health*, Winter 2019, https://www.hsph.harvard.edu/magazine/ magazine_article/america-is-failing-its-black-mothers/.

20 Lawrence B. Finer, Lori F. Frohwirth, Lindsay A. Dauphinee, Susheela Singh, and Ann M. Moore, "Reasons U.S. Women Have Abortions: Quantitative and Qualitative Perspectives," *Perspectives on Sexual and Reproductive Health* 37, no. 3 (September 2005): 110–18, https://www.guttmacher.org/sites/default/files/pdfs/ journals/3711005.pdf.

21 Read more and find out how to get involved in advocacy in your state at endthebacklog.org.

22 "LGBTQ Americans Aren't Fully Protected From Discrimination in 30 States," freedomforallamericans.org.

23 "The Lies and Dangers of Efforts to Change Sexual Orientation or Gender Identity," Human Rights Campaign, September 6, 2011, https://www.hrc.org/resources/the-lies-and-dangers-of-reparative- therapy.

24 "Exodus International Shuts Down: Christian Ministry Apologizes to LGBT Community and Halts Operations," Huffington Post, updated December 6, 2017, https://www.huffpost.com/entry/ exodus-international-shuts-down_n_3470911.

THE AUTHOR

Megan K. Westra is on the pastoral staff team at Transformation City Church in Milwaukee, Wisconsin. A dynamic and passionate public speaker, Westra presented at the Christian Community Development Association's national conference in 2015 and 2017. Westra is pursuing her MDiv at Northern Seminary. She lives in Milwaukee with her husband of eight years, Ben, and their six-year-old daughter, Cadence.